ietting' In & Getting' Out

ow to Get In Every Prospect's Door and Gei

MU01064717

cond Printing
inted in the United States of America
BN: 978-0-9815657-0-5
us058000 Business / Sales & Selling
brary of Congress Catalog Number: 2006930108
9.95 U.S. Funds
2.95 CAN Funds

iblished by:

iccess Starts Now
51 Atrium Way
ashville, TN 37214
ione: 877-589-0606 ext.704
ix: 615-884-3370

anufactured under the direction of **FRP**

division of Southwestern/Great American, Inc.
ashville, Tennessee

over Design --- Travis Rader

Dedication

To my mother, Judy Siegel, and my father, Bob Michels, for raising me to be a successful and efficient member of our society. Both of them have taught me the values and ethics I have today.

Acknowledgements

This book is an accumulation and consolidation of the best ideas, techniques, and strategies I have learned, practiced, and perfected over my twenty-three year sales career. I am indebted to several people for their assistance, advice, and encouragement related to this book and my sales career.

A special thanks goes out to Dawn Josephson of Cameo Publications for her help week after week editing this book and making my writing look great. And to Amanda Finney for helping me create the awesome cover. To both of you…Cheers!

I would like to express my gratitude to Tom McAuliffe of the Southwestern Company, who pushed me to be the best I could be when I was just a college student selling reference books door-to-door in the summer time. My three summers in the Southwestern program served as the foundation to my success today.

I would also like to thank the following people at Great American Opportunities Inc., all of whom I have admired, learned from, and became friends with during my nineteen very special years with the company: Craig Hill, Keith Hill, Rick Garlock, Stacy Stibbe, Tim Haskins, Tim Fish, Ricky Grice, Randy Grice, Marc Hamilton, Derek Garza, Phil McLeod, Marc Peters, Carrie Gehlhausen, Cheri Schraeder, Jeff Peterson, Gary Pears, and so many others that it would take forever to mention.

I had two managers who believed in me and gave me the opportunity to excel, as well as an opportunity to lead others—something that is very important to me in life. I would first like to thank Vinod Chopra for his support and friendship over all the years as we built a strong team out in California, and I would like to thank Kevin Hawley for his leadership skills that he passed on to me.

One of the most influential people in my life is Tom McDow, who is the current CEO of Great American Opportunities. Tom had such a wonderful way of letting me know that he cared about me and my success. He taught me how to be a responsible, professional leader in all areas of my life. Tom, thank you for your blessing.

I would also like express gratitude to Henry Bedford, Ralph Mosley, and Spencer Hays of the Southwestern Company for believing in me and partnering with me to build the new Motivational Speaking and Training Division of our company that is called Success Starts Now!

Special appreciation goes out to Lee Milteer, my speaking coach. Lee inspired me and taught me how to go about writing this book. Her frankness and coaching style really made a difference in who I am today.

There have been numerous times over the years when I needed something special done for me in my business. I would like to give special thanks to Cindy Schulkins and Tina Welch for all the times they were there for me.

Several people allowed me to pick their brains about their business philosophy and their sales techniques, and some of them actually allowed me to spend time traveling with them in their territory and better learning what they do. I am forever grateful to Lori Rappa (Selling Power), Ben Volkman (Baseline Balance and Performance), Joe Walsh (American Wireless), Scott Robbins (Cyberhome), Joel Mostert (Heger Realty), Collier Granberry (San Jose Magazine), Gary Cruff (Ameriprise), Rudy Caparros (California Chemical), Whit Behrens (Tom James Clothing Company), and Terry Meyer and Chris Hawkins (Intero Real Estate Services). Thank you all.

I would like to also say thank you to Terry Brennan and Matt Biggs, two of my best friends who have always been there for me through thick and thin.

Of course I would like to thank my family for their support: my brother Grant, his wife Debbie, my two nephews Noah and Leo, my sister Rachel, my mother Judy Siegel, and my father Bob Michels. I know you are all very proud of me.

I would also like to give a big thank you to the following people who are right there by my side helping me build the best company ever in Success

Starts Now! Thank you goes out to Henry Bedford, Cindy Johnstone, Mary Miller, Dan Moore, Jerry Heffel, Spencer Hays, Dustin Hillis, Kyah Hillis, Rory Vaden, Amanda Johns, Paul Schween, Lois Francis, Fatima Michels, Marc Savas, Steve Reiner, Jeff Heath, Lars Tewes, and Ryan Tabor.

And last but not least, I would like to thank the love of my life, my wife, Fatima, and her son, Brandon, for their unconditional love and support for me. Fatima, you have been so supportive in the whole process of writing this book and starting the new company, Success Starts Now! Honey, I love and thank you dearly.

Contents

Foreword

I have known Gary Michels for all of the twenty years of his professional career in sales. As a college student, Gary worked during the summers in the student sales and sales training internship program of The Southwestern Company in Nashville Tennessee, selling books on a door-to-door basis to pay for his school tuition. He became a top producer, ranking in the top one percent (actually the top half of the top one percent) among the 3,000 students selling across the country, and returned to sell for a second and third summer. Gary made enough money to graduate from The University of California, Santa Barbara with his tuition paid and money in the bank.

After graduation, Gary interned with Great American Opportunities, at that time a new subsidiary of Southwestern in the school fundraising business. Gary joined the company on a full time basis in 1988 after his final summer with Southwestern. As Great American grew in stature, eventually becoming the second largest fundraising company in America, Gary led the way. He was the top sales representative seven out of the last ten years of his career with Great American, and always in the top five of the two hundred fifty person national sales force.

During his years at Great American, Gary was invited to speak on numerous occasions regarding his formula for success, grounded in the Southwestern experience. He developed a passion for teaching others the principles that have been proven to be instrumental in his rise to the top. On his own time he sought out and developed mentoring relationships with other top sellers in a dozen other industries, not as teacher but as student. He traveled with these top professionals, following them to the field and observing first hand their techniques, their successes, and their failures. He discovered that the fundamental principles that defined his success and Southwestern's success were timeless and applicable to any selling situation.

In December of 2005, Gary entered into an agreement with Southwestern and a number of other partners to start Success Starts Now, a public speaking and training company aimed at helping sales professionals achieve extraordinary sales execution, and helping people of all walks of life achieve success. The company hosts training events in major cities across the country, and provides a suite of products for individuals and companies including longer term training curriculums, sales consulting, coaching, and self help materials.

Gettin' In & Gettin' Out is Gary Michels' written prescription for personal success in selling. It outlines the techniques, disciplines, self-talk, and habits that lead to extraordinary results in sales execution. I encourage you to spend time in these pages, not only reading about the principles involved, but taking the time to internalize the habits that have allowed one of the nation's top sellers to make small work out of challenging and seemingly impossible sales situations.

   – Henry Bedford, Chairman and CEO, Southwestern/Great American Inc.

Introduction

According to a recent study reported in *Selling Power* magazine, seventy percent of America's workforce does the absolute minimum at work. They drag themselves into the office late, leave early, take long breaks, and do just enough to keep the boss happy and *not* get fired. Twenty percent of our workforce does less than minimum, and as a result they move from job to job. Only a mere ten percent of today's workers do more than average on the job.

Well, if you're reading this book, then congratulations, because you are among that ten percent. You are learning, trying to better yourself, and striving to be a true success in one of the toughest yet most fun professions in the world—sales.

Being a sales professional, you likely hear people tell you almost constantly that you have lots of competition. But if you look at the numbers, you really don't. Remember, you're in the ten percent who does more than average. The other ninety percent who do average or below average at work don't hold a candle to you, so they're really not your competition. In fact, over the years, I have witnessed that our biggest competition is usually the person looking back at us in the mirror. That's right; *you* are your biggest competitor. That's why the concepts in this book will not show you how to be cutthroat, ruthless, and beat the other guy or gal out of a sale. Rather, I'm going to show you how to be the best of the best in the sales profession by working on yourself so you rise to the top of the ten percent category—so you win the sale without resorting to sales games.

Realize that no matter where you currently are in your sales career, you can improve. If you're just starting out, the concepts in this book will kick-start your efforts so you can reach the ranks of the top producers quicker and easier. If you're already at the top producer level, you'll learn some creative strategies that will make your job even easier. And if you're somewhere in the middle, you'll discover techniques that will shave years off your learning curve and enable you to reach your goals sooner.

Okay, So Why Listen to Me?

Before we get into the meat of the matter, let me tell you a bit about myself and why I'm qualified to reveal these sales techniques.

I'm proud to say that I have been in sales my entire life. My friends and family often joke that I came out of the womb asking, "Ya wanna buy a book?"

As a young teen I was the top newspaper carrier in the region for the *San Jose Mercury News*. I was up at 5:00 a.m. every morning to deliver newspapers. When I got a little older, I was involved in just about every network marketing company in existence and sold everything from security products to vitamins. And yes, I made money doing this.

While in college I did the usual summer jobs: waiting tables and delivering pizza. Then, one spring day during the end of my sophomore year at University of California, Santa Barbara, I saw an ad in the school newspaper that read: "Make $5,500 average this summer." The ad said there was an informational meeting that evening in the church right next to my fraternity house. Sure, it sounded too good to be true, but I thought, *"What the heck? I could be rich!"* So I went to the meeting.

The gentleman running the meeting was from The Southwestern Company out of Nashville, TN. He explained that we would be selling reference books, and that successful salespeople work thirteen and a half hours per day, six days a week. He also said it would be door-to-door sales.

At this point, most of the people at the meeting left. But I was intrigued.

Then he said, "When you get to your destination city, you have to find a place to live."

"What do you mean?" I asked. "Don't I sell here in Santa Barbara, or back in San Jose, where I live?"

"No," he replied. "Once school gets out for the summer you will pack yourself in a car with three or four other people and drive directly out to Nashville. It's a forty hour drive. Then you'll go through an intensive one-week sales training program before you head out to your headquarters, somewhere in New England. While in training, you will train thirteen and a half hours a day and stay outside all day except when you go to the bathroom. Oh, and, by the way, while in training you'll stay at a cheap motel, take cold showers every morning to get yourself pumped and motivated, and sing a crazy song called *The Bookman's Song.*"

Now I was really intrigued.

"Okay," I said. "How much money can I expect to make?"

"Didn't you read the newspaper ad?" he asked.

"Of course. It said $5,500 was average. But I'm better than average."

"Well, the truth is that a lot of people quit after the first few days and fly home. Others do less than average but don't quit. Many students do the average or a bit more. And a handful makes $20,000, $30,000, and even $40,000 in just one summer."

I had always been the odd one in the family. And while most people would run away from such a proposition, I simply asked, "Where do I sign up?"

It's amazing how a one hour long meeting can change your life forever. I sold Southwestern books for three summers and made over $80,000 doing so—a great amount of money for a college student in the late 1980s. I finished in the top half percent of over three thousand college students worldwide, and I paid my entire way through four years of college. I even had a little money left over to upgrade from my 1972 Ford Pinto to a fully loaded Toyota Forerunner Truck. Not too bad for a kid just entering the real working world.

During the time I spent selling books, I learned and refined the essential skills of being a master sales person. I've heard people say that we are the Navy Seals of selling.

One benefit of selling books for The Southwestern Company is that they have a job placement center and can help you find a sales career after your book selling career is over. So I met with Carl Roberts, the director of the placement center. He told me about a sales job with Great American Opportunities Inc., a company that helped schools and youth organizations raise money through the sale of different products, such as wrapping paper, candy, cookie dough, discount cards, etc.

He explained that I would use the sales skills I learned selling books to sell fundraising products to teachers and administrators, and that I'd get to use the skills I learned from my experiences in community theatre to do motivational presentations to the students, getting them fired up to sell and make a ton of money for their school or organization, such as cheerleading, football, academic clubs, etc.

It sounded like a fun job, so I decided to give it a try.

Nineteen years later I left the industry having broken every sales record imaginable. The four accomplishments I'm most proud of are: 1) Shipping over $1 million worth of product in one year, which helped schools raise over $800,000 for their various organizations. 2) Over the course of my career, raising over $7.5 million profit for schools, which paid for things like field trips, scholarships, uniforms, coaches, playground equipment, etc. 3) Being the number one sales rep in our company out of 250 sales reps nationwide. I was fortunate to do this nine of the nineteen years I was with the company. And 4) Getting the opportunity to speak to over 700,000 students and teachers over the years and making a difference in their lives.

That fourth point is perhaps the most important to me, because in life we have several opportunities to make a difference for others. I learned that lesson through personal experience one fall day. In the late 1990s I was working at a large elementary school in Milpitas CA. During my assembly I asked for a volunteer to come up and help me with a magic trick I used to demonstrate to the kids how to sell. A young girl, around ten years old, waved her hand and jumped up and down, so I called her on up. We had a blast together. We laughed and joked around, and she did great. After the assembly, my client came up to me crying.

"Why are you crying" I asked with a lot of concern.

She said, "Today was that young girl's first day back at school in a month. Both of her parents died in an automobile accident a month ago. I know the family very well. Today was the first day I have seen her smile since the accident. Thanks so much for making a difference."

Every day we choose whether or not to make a difference. It does not matter what you sell or what you do, you still have that choice. By choosing to always strive to get better in all aspects of your life, personal and business, you are making a difference in your life and the lives of those around you

You have such a choice right now. You can choose to keep doing what you have always been doing, or you can choose to try something new—something that you learn in this book.

To Be the Best, Learn from the Best

Besides my personal sales experiences, I have spent much time "in the field" watching several different sales professionals at work. I spent time with sales professionals in various industries, including financial, real estate, advertising, technology, retail, electronics, clothing sales, and several others. In addition to observing how they handle real-life selling situations, I also interviewed them about what worked, what didn't work, and what they wished they had more training in.

I asked them such questions as:

- What do the top producers in your industry do?

- What are your daily goals?

- How do you prospect?

- What keeps you awake at night?

- If you had to produce 1/12 of your yearly goal in just one week, what would you do?

- How do you establish rapport and how important is it?

- What is your average day look like?

- Do you follow a sales talk or presentation for answering objections, or do you wing it?

- How do you close for the sale?

- Do you trial close?

- How big a part of your business are referrals?

- Tell me about your biggest sale ever.

- How have you used what you've learned to continue growing your business?

Their answers amazed me. Even though the people I met with were from completely different industries and sold very different products and services, some universal truths emerged—truths we're going to cover in this book. These truths from these top producers didn't involve beating the competition down to make themselves look good, as many sales books tell you to do; rather, these top producers focused on themselves—getting better at their career so they could naturally get more business. By focusing on improving themselves rather than putting someone else down, they made a positive impact on their lives and the lives of everyone they interacted with.

If this sounds like the approach you want to take, then read on. We have lots of ground to cover, so let's get started…

Chapter One

The Keys of Gettin' In and Gettin' Out

Let's begin by addressing the concept of "Gettin' In" and "Gettin' Out." What do those phrases mean in terms of the sales profession?

When I use these phrases in my workshops and seminars, some people think it has something to do with In and Out Burger. A teeny, tiny percentage actually thinks it has something to do with porn. Both are way off.

Gettin' In means getting yourself in a position where you have a captive audience who will listen to you and consider purchasing what you have to sell. It means doing the legwork to find out who the decision makers are. In sales, we typically call this the pre-approach. It's all about getting the appointment! So Gettin' In means developing the proper mindset, planning, setting goals, and prospecting so you get your desired result: A PRESENTATION!

Phil Schneider, the current sales record holder for Great American Opportunities, says, "Gettin' In means you're setting up the opportunity to leave the door open for future sales year after year. Then, once the door is open, you treat your clients well so other doors open for you via referrals."

But Gettin' In is only half the equation. You then need the Gettin' Out part.

Gettin' Out means leaving the prospect's office with a signed contract or purchase order, or at the very least, advancing yourself in the sales process and moving closer to a final possible "yes" answer. It means winning the deal and getting the sale. It's all about knowing the behavioral style of the person you're meeting with, making a great first impression, building rapport, going through the various parts of the sales presentation (the sales talk, the corral, the pre-sell, the product presentation, the add-on, and the close), overcoming objections, closing the deal, and then getting referrals for future opportunities.

Whit Behrens, one of the top producers for the Tom James Personal Clothing Company, says that Gettin' In and Gettin' Out as quickly and efficiently as possible, and in as many situations as possible, is key to his success. For example, if he has a noon, 2:00 p.m., and 4:00 p.m. appointment, he must still build rapport with each person. But instead of doing it by just sitting and making small talk, he builds rapport as he's fitting his client's clothing. He respects their time by not taking too long and getting out, and respects his other appointment's time by not being late and getting in. So he gets in and gets out by focusing on respect and personal responsibility.

Why Gettin' In and Gettin' Out Are Often So Difficult

For many people, sales is a hard profession to pursue for the long term. In fact, recent findings indicate that thirty-five to forty percent of new salespeople leave the profession their first year. That's a huge attrition rate. But if people can make it past that critical first year, their chances for success greatly improve. For example, while I was at Great American Opportunities, we found that if a salesperson was there for three years, he or she would stay long term. But those first three years were the most critical.

What dominates new salespeople's thinking that first year? Self-doubt. People doubt themselves and their ability to produce at a high level. They wonder how they'll get everything done, how they'll stay motivated and on task, how they'll get in front of more people and close them, and how they'll really make it in the sales profession.

And the biggest reason why people have these thoughts is a lack of training. That's where this book will help!

When you understand and implement the concepts in this book, any concerns, fears, or self-doubt you have will disappear. Why? Because the concepts in this book focus on changing and maintaining you, not your prospect or your company, but you. Think about it…You cannot control other people or events. But you can control yourself and the actions you take. What you say and how you act, if done effectively, will enable you to achieve your desired results. If you learn the skills and techniques I outline in this book, *and use them regularly*, you will become confident when selling. As a result, you will more regularly experience success. As this happens, your concerns and fears will naturally go away, because confidence and fear are on opposite ends of the emotional spectrum.

How to Use This Book

To get the most results from this book, I recommend you do the following:

◆ First, take notes *in* the book. Yes, actually write in the margins or in the Notes sections provided.

◆ Consolidate your notes onto one typed page, front and back.

◆ Print out and laminate this sheet of notes.

◆ Keep the sheet of notes in your car or briefcase.

◆ Read these notes at least twice per day for twenty-one days, and then once per day for the next several days until you really believe the subject matter is a part of your natural process.

◆ During your reading period, jump right in and try two new techniques a week.

◆ Once you feel that you have made progress in the two new techniques, try two more.

◆ Continue for three months. If you're compelled to continue for another three months, please go ahead and do so.

◆ If you need further training in any area, you can get additional training from many different companies, including ours, Southwestern Business Resources. To find out if we can help you, call 1-877-589-0606 extension 704.

If you follow the process just outlined, you'll be able to better use your time. You'll be a well rounded person, both personally and professionally. You'll get in more sales doors, thereby giving you more chances to make a sale and earn a higher income—two things I rarely hear salespeople complain about. You'll learn to work smarter and harder at the same time, yet you'll learn how to fit this into a balanced lifestyle.

If you incorporate the principles I outline in this book into your daily life, you should be able to double your income in the next two years. Yes, I said "double your income in two years." But you have to follow my techniques exactly. Realize that accomplishing this may mean hiring an assistant, which I explain how to do in this book; it may even mean changing companies if your current company's compensation plan doesn't allow for the numbers you'd like to hit. But when you sit down and give some deep thought into how you can use the techniques and concepts that you'll learn in this book to double your income in the next two years, you'll see that the tools are here for your taking.

Get Ready to Get In, Get Out, and Get Rich

I wrote this book in a way that touches on all the key areas of the sales process. You'll see actual examples of specific verbiage to use with prospects and creative ways to get in more sales doors. As a result, you'll experience better results than you are currently getting. I've created a mix of techniques and motivation— something most salespeople tell me is important. It's this finely balanced mix that gets people to take action.

So are you ready to change your life? Are you ready for explosive results? Are you ready to become a top producing salesperson who gets in every prospect's door and gets out with a sale? Then let's begin by helping you develop the proper mindset. Read on to find out how.

Section One

Gettin' In

Chapter Two

Develop the Proper Mindset

I
f you want to be a top producer who knows how to get in every prospect's door and get out with a sale, then you must have the mindset of a top producer.

What's your mindset? Do you have the mindset of a top producer, or is your mindset more like the ninety percent of people in the workforce? Take this quick quiz to find out.

Mindset Self-Assessment

For each question, pick the answer that best describes you.

1. When it comes to training, I have the proper training (both from the company and from external sources I seek out) to excel at my job.

    a. <u>Completely agree.</u> I take advantage of every company training program and I go out and seek outside training and coaching on a regular basis.

    b. <u>Somewhat agree.</u> I take advantage of a few internal and external training and coaching options, but not as many as I'd like.

    c.   <u>Disagree</u>. I don't take advantage of many if any company training programs or outside training options because I'm simply too busy to bother.

2. I have a clearly defined work ethic that keeps me on task and free from excuses as to why I can't produce the numbers I need.

    a.   <u>Completely agree</u>. I have my personal work ethic written out and posted in a spot where I can review it daily. I live by my work ethic.

    b.   <u>Somewhat agree</u>. I mentally know what my work ethic is and I usually let it dictate my daily activities and decisions.

    c.   <u>Disagree</u>. I never actually outlined my work ethic and don't use one to guide my daily activities and decisions.

3. I am completely accountable for reaching my goals.

    a.   <u>Completely agree</u>. I share my goals with others and do whatever it takes to reach my goals.

    b.   <u>Somewhat agree</u>. I reach many of my goals. But if I miss some, that's okay. No one's perfect, after all.

    c.   <u>Disagree</u>. I have a few goals I want to reach. If I reach them this year or next year or whenever, that's fine. I'm not on any real time table.

4. The people I associate with and hang out with push me to succeed and help keep me on task. They are go-getters and top producers themselves.

    a.   <u>Completely agree</u>. The people I hang out with are my inspiration. They are more successful than me and motivate me to continually do better.

    b.   <u>Somewhat agree</u>. The people I hang out with are at the same level as me. A few may be a little more driven and a few may be a little less. But all in all, we balance each other out.

    c.   <u>Disagree</u>. The people I hang out with are at the same level or slightly below me success wise.

5. I live a life that balances the seven main areas of life: Physical, Spiritual, Mental, Financial, Social, Family, and Career.

    a. <u>Completely agree</u>. I do whatever I can to ensure I'm giving equal attention to all seven life areas, and I often succeed at keeping a good balance.

    b. <u>Somewhat agree</u>. I try to stay balanced, but I don't always succeed. Something from one area or another always seems to dominate my attention and throw me off balance.

    c. <u>Disagree</u>. I regularly ignore a few areas of my life so I can have gains in the other areas. I'll have plenty of time later to focus on the areas I'm ignoring today.

6. I keep my mindset positive by using positive affirmations and thinking positive thoughts.

    a. <u>Completely agree</u>. I have a list of positive affirmations that I say daily, and I do whatever I can to keep my mind focused on positive thoughts.

    b. <u>Somewhat agree</u>. I don't have an actual list of affirmations that I say, but I do try to be an optimist and think positive thoughts.

    c. <u>Disagree</u>. I don't have time for this positive affirmation stuff. My life is way too busy to repeat silly phrases to myself or to think warm, fuzzy thoughts.

Now add up how many of each answer you have—how many As, Bs, and Cs.

A._____ B._____ C. _____

If you answered mostly A answers, then you definitely have the top producer mindset. You are probably very successful in sales, but you still have one or two challenges that you struggle with. Keep reading so you can reach even higher levels of success.

If you answered mostly B answers, then you are close to being a top producer. You are relatively successful in sales, but you struggle more than necessary to maintain your current level, not to mention to advance to better and bigger things. Keep reading so you can fine-tune your processes and work smarter rather than harder.

If you answered mostly C answers, then you are either brand new to sales or you are not properly trained in what it takes to be a top producer. You have limited success in your field, and are often frustrated watching everyone else scores the big deals while you struggle to get a single appointment. Keep reading so you can discover what it really takes to reach the top producer level.

Regardless of how you scored, realize that top producers see the world very differently. They have a unique mindset that puts them at the top. Fortunately, with a little patience and persistence, you can adopt their mindset.

Invest in Number One

Top producers invest in themselves. They love to accumulate information that will help them get better in any way possible. They read daily, even if it is just for five minutes, and they listen to motivational and educations tapes and CDs in their car. I call my car "CU"—Car University. I listen to motivational CDs as I drive to the office to set the tone for a positive day. I get so much energy from this learning time that people say I make coffee nervous. But most people like to see and be around positive energy.

In addition to reading and listening to CDs, top producers attend an average of two seminars per year that are above and beyond what their company provides for them in training. These can be on various topics, from planning and goal setting to financial planning and prospecting. Seriously consider going outside your company for additional training, because doing so gives you a new perspective on things and enables you to get in contact with new people for networking purposes. Who knows…you may find your next big client at one of these seminars.

To find a seminar or outside training suitable for you, ask some of the top producers in your company what outside training seminars they attend of course, I would suggest you go to one our **Success Starts Now** seminars (www. ssnowseminars.com. Also, you can do an Internet search of possible seminars, and check the community pages of your local newspaper. You can also join e-mail lists of companies who offer such trainings. Then when one is coming to your area, you'll get a notification. Additionally, be sure to regularly visit your local bookstore. Browse the new arrivals for books and CDs that would benefit you.

Finally, top producers often invest in personal and business coaching. I have had two coaches recently, one for motivational speaking and the other for real estate. The accountability and support a coach provides is priceless. After all, you're paying for this person's time and expertise; you're not going to waste your money by not listening to what the person says or not doing what the person suggests.

Realize that you don't have to go "full boar" with your coaching and agree to a two year coaching contract that costs hundreds of thousands of dollars. You can do one coaching session only. Sure, you can fully immerse yourself in coaching, but that's not always necessary or possible. The key is to simply learn good information and habits from someone more successful than you—someone you aspire to be like.

Additionally, when you work with a coach, even if it's just for one session, you gain immediate access to a whole network of top producers and potential top producers. Chances are your coach is working with more people than just you. That means you can learn from all these other people's experiences, and possibly network with them in the future. Now you have access to a wealth of information beyond what the coach offers.

Finally, coaches offer a different perspective than your manager. While you may be hesitant to tell your manager something for fear of committing professional suicide, you can feel comfortable telling your coach these things. Coaches are not there to judge you; they listen and offer guidance in a non-judgmental way, with the goal of helping you become better.

Top producers have a consistent thirst for knowledge that enables them to compete and win in the marketplace, not only today, but also in the future. Sure, it takes time, money, and commitment to devote yourself to a path of self improvement. But top producers know that the payoff far exceeds the cost.

The legendary sales trainer Brian Tracy once said that you should invest as much in yourself and your professional growth each year as you do in the service and upkeep of your car. For some of you with the fancy upscale automobiles, that's a lot of money, but don't worry. The investment is worth it. And for those of you who drive the 1972 Pinto and change your own oil, you might want to ask yourself, "Why is that? Why am I not driving a better car?"

I am personally investing over $5,000 in myself this year. I'm taking a year-long class on "How to be a Better Motivational Speaker," I'm working with a coach, I'm attending seminars, and I'm buying books and tapes. And because all of this is tax deductible, the investment isn't as big as the number actually seems.

If you're wondering where you'll come up with the money for educational pursuit, figure how much you make from each sale. Then do enough "extra" sales to cover the cost of the personal investment. While I worked at Great American Opportunities, I figured that all I needed to do to pay for my yearly education was close two extra deals. That's not much at all.

So start changing your mindset to that of a top producer by identifying where you would invest this money. What seminars would you attend? What books or CDs would you purchase? Who would you seek advice from? Get clear on this so you can take steps in the right direction.

Work it Right

Top producers have an excellent work ethic. They are totally disciplined to stay on track, no matter what.

What does a good work ethic look like? People with a good work ethic set deadlines and goals for themselves, and they don't quit until they achieve them. They work eight to ten hours per day, five days a week, and a bit more on Sunday night so they can prepare for the following week. People with a good work ethic put in forty to fifty hours per week, sometimes more when a special project requires extra attention. At the office, they don't let the resident "chit-chatter" distract them from their daily tasks. They work hard, but they play hard, too.

I often read a book called *The Common Denominator* by Albert Gray. The key sentence in that book—the sentence that I live by—is this: "The secret of success for every person who has been successful lies in the fact that he or she has formed the habits of doing things that failures don't like to do." That's work ethic!

When I think of good work ethic, I think of Barry Bonds of the San Francisco Giants. A lot of people think he is an absolute jerk, but I admire his ability to stay focused and achieve his maximum potential. I sit next to his wife Liz at Pac ATT Park (or at least that's what it's called now—it has changed names so many times). I asked her, "What does Barry do in the off season?"

She replied, "What off season? He doesn't have an off season, like most of his teammates do. Two weeks after the season ends, Barry works out with his trainer eight hours a day to stay in top form for the following year. He does not work on getting back in shape; he stays in shape!"

Are there areas in your professional life where you act like a warm bed slug? Where you slack off because others do it? Where you let your work ethic slide because you feel entitled to do so? If there were a hidden camera watching everything you did during your work day and your parents, spouse, children, best friends, and boss were watching, would they be proud to say they are affiliated with you?

Take a few moments and write down what's important to you in terms of working for success. What kinds of things do you want to do on a daily basis? What kind of things do you want to avoid? What kind of things will propel you to success? These bullet points that you write out is your personal work ethic. These are the points you want to commit to no matter what.

On a regular basis (monthly at the very least) examine your personal definition of a good work ethic. Are you true to it? If so, how can you still improve? If not, what can you do to change? Develop a strong work ethic so you can rise to the top.

Accountability Matters

Top producers have a thorough understanding of both personal and business accountability. They prospect, set goals, practice their scripts, and follow up with clients—even when they don't feel like it. Top producers don't make excuses as to why they can't succeed; rather, they look for a solution to the challenge that's holding them back.

For example, while I worked at Great American Opportunities, I often interviewed prospective salespeople. One interviewee, Tammy Schaeffer, really blew my socks off with her level of accountability.

During the interview, Tammy asked me what the sales record was for a first year sales rep. I told her. She then said to me, "Well watch out, because I'm not just going to hit that mark, but I'm also going to break it. If you hire me and hold me accountable to that goal, I'll do it." I was so impressed that I hired her.

Throughout the year she continually showed me her charts, graphs, and plans, and I held up my end of the bargain by keeping her accountable to her goal. At year's end, while she didn't hit the goal, she did come incredibly close and ended the year in the number two position. During her first year with Great American Opportunities, she earned over $100,000—double of what the typical first year sales rep earns. And it was her level of accountability that enabled her to do that.

Similarly, we had a single dad on our sales team. Now, I've never had the experience of being a single dad, but I know it must be extremely difficult to balance your work and your children's needs. I also know that when a child gets sick, he or she often needs the loving touch only a parent can give to feel better. As a result, it would have been very easy for this single dad to use his sick child as an excuse for not reaching goals.

However, this particular salesperson found a way to overcome this excuse. If his child got sick, he found a way to still prospect and follow up and reach his goals. Sometimes he worked from home so he could care for his sick child, sometimes he found a sitter or family member to watch the child, or sometimes he took the day off but worked extra hard the other days to catch up. Whatever solution he found, he made sure he stayed on track while not neglecting his child. I was always awed by his dedication and ability to achieve such balance. He was so accountable to his goals and himself that he came up with some very creative solutions to ensure he stayed on task.

I recently read a story that happened to a businessman who was eating lunch at a restaurant. The gentleman was in a hurry to get back to the office, yet the waiter never came to take his order. So the businessman stopped the busboy and asked him if he could take the order. Although the busboy had a full tray of dishes in his hand, he agreed to take the man's order.

"I'll have a salad, two rolls, and a diet Coke," the man said.

"We don't have diet Coke," the busboy replied. "Would diet Pepsi be okay?"

"No thank you. Just bring me water with lemon then."

A couple minutes later, the busboy brought out the salad, two rolls, and water. Three minutes later, the busboy returned with an ice cold diet Coke.

Surprised, the man said, "What's this? How did you get the diet Coke? I thought you don't carry it."

"I asked my manager to run next door to the grocery store and get it for you," said the busboy.

A few months later when the man went back to the restaurant, the busboy was nowhere to be found. The man learned that the young employee had been promoted to a manager at another location.

When in the busboy's shoes, many people would have asked, "Why do I have to do all the work around here?" or "Who is supposed to be covering this section?" or "Why don't we carry diet Coke?" These are simply excuses for not doing the work that needs to get done. When you do this, you're giving yourself reasons not to be accountable.

We all fall into the trap of making excuses at some point in our lives. Recently I had a cast on my arm and kept making the excuse that I can't fix the filter of the Koi pond with only one arm. Of course I could fix it with one arm, but I was making an excuse and not being accountable.

The bottom line is that we all make excuses all the time. We make excuses for not working hard enough, not prospecting, not practicing, etc. Top producers don't make excuses; they just do what needs to be done, and they don't complain about it. They're accountable for everything they must do.

If you want to enhance your accountability mindset, read the book *The Question Behind the Question* by John Miller. If you take notes about this book the way I described earlier, you will be on your way to becoming more accountable.

Think of accountability this way: If no one was around you, would you still get things done? That's accountability.

Birds of a Feather...

Top producers tend to become like the people they associate with. Are the people around you and the people you seek knowledge from contributing to or taking away from your power to succeed in your profession?

In the real estate profession, the top agents get together often in what's called a Mastermind Group. These high powered professionals use this time to share ideas of what's working and what's not working. Similarly, while I was with Great American, I was part of the Chairman's Club, which is a high powered group of top producing sales people. We vacationed together, golfed together, did conference calls together, etc. Basically, we fed off of each other's positive attitude.

Never seek advice from someone who is less successful than you. Additionally, if your co-workers, family, or friends are not a positive influence on you, then you need to avoid them at all costs. I know it is difficult to do this with family, but you must address it and not brush it under the rug. Be upfront with these people and tell them that you have set some high standards for yourself and you don't have room for negativity in your life at this time.

If you want to be doing as well as the top producers in your company, seek them out! Don't be shy. Seek them out and ask if you can have some phone time with them. Ask them if you can take them to lunch and pick their brains. Ask if you can do a ride along and cross train with them. The worst thing they can say to you is "no." And if they do, so what? Simply ask somebody else who is doing well in your company or industry. Be persistent and it'll pay off.

Here's an example of how persistence can pay off: About five years ago I really wanted to take my public speaking to the next level. I told myself that I needed to speak with the best! I had seen Tom Hopkins speak on several occasions and read most of his books. He was, and still is, one of the masters when it comes to sales techniques. I decided to call him and see if he would give me a few minutes of his time. I was even willing to fly to Arizona to speak with him and do whatever I needed to do to have a few minutes of his time.

So I called his office and asked to speak with him. His secretary gave me the usual blow off and said, "People who want speaking advice all get the same answer. Tom says that you should get involved with the National Speakers Association."

"I already am involved," I said. "I go to several of their events each year. I have read most of Tom's books, and I've seen him speak several times. All I want is a few minutes of phone time or some in person time with him."

She said, "Tom doesn't return calls like this because he gets so many requests."

I continued, "Tell me, does Tom drive to work each day?"

"Yes," she said.

"Does he eat breakfast?"

"Well of course."

"Great," I said. "I really would like to talk to Tom on the phone or in person, even if I have to fly to Arizona and wait in the parking lot with breakfast in my hand. At least then I'd have his attention for those few minutes while he walks from his car into the building."

I could tell the secretary was impressed with my persistence.

She then said, "I will see what I can do, but I can't promise anything."

A few weeks passed by and I had completely forgotten about my request. Then my cell phone rang.

The husky voice on the line said, "Gary Michels?"

"Yes," I said.

"Tom Hopkins, here. I understand you have some questions for me."

We spent the next half hour on the phone. During the call Tom complimented me on my parking lot meeting technique and gave me a lot of good advice that I still use today. By the way, this parking lot technique works great when you really need to speak with the big decision maker. I have used it several times over the years.

The bottom line is to do whatever you must to associate with the kind of people who can help you with your career. Get into the professional circles that will energize you and support you as you set and reach new goals for yourself.

Get Balanced

Top producers tend to live a balanced lifestyle. They are not perfect, but they are always striving for perfection in the seven main areas of their life: Physical, Spiritual, Mental, Financial, Social, Family, and Career.

How do you rate in these seven areas of life? How balanced are you? To find out, do this quick exercise:

On a scale of 1 to 10, with 10 being the highest, rate yourself on the following Key Factors in each area. If the particular factor does not apply to you, simply write NA (not applicable) in the space.

Physical

_____ Appearance

_____ Regular check-up

_____ Energy level

_____ Planned recreation & relaxation

_____ Sports participation

_____ Regular fitness program

_____ Weight control

_____ Diet & nutrition

_____ Stress control

_____ Cardiovascular endurance

_____ Total divided by 10 = _____

Spiritual

_____ Belief in God or Higher Power

_____ Inner peace

_____ Influence on others

_____ Spouse/Significant other relationship

_____ Church/Temple involvement

_____ Sense of purpose

_____ Positive attitude toward giving

_____ Prayer/Bible study/meditation

_____ Charitable work

_____ Sharing with others

_____ Total divided by 10 = _____

Mental

_____ Attitude

_____ Intelligence

_____ Formal education

_____ Continuing education & training

_____ Creative imagination

_____ Inspirational reading

_____ CD/Cassette tape/ DVD education

_____ Inquisitive mind

_____ Enthusiasm

_____ Self-image

_____ Total divided by 10 = _____

Financial

_____ Prosperity priority

_____ Personal budget

_____ Avoids impulse purchases

_____ Earnings

_____ Living within income

_____ Minimal charge accounts

_____ Adequate insurance

_____ Investments

_____ Retirement savings

_____ Savings

_____ Total divided by 10 = _____

Social

_____ Ease at gatherings

_____ Courteous nature

_____ Avoids gossip

_____ Positive sense of humor

_____ Self-confidence

_____ Community activities

_____ Praises others

_____ Good listener

_____ Friendly

_____ Good personal hygiene

_____ Total divided by 10 = _____

Family

_____ Good listening habits

_____ Good role model

_____ Takes vacations

_____ Forgiving attitude

_____ Builds self-esteem in others

_____ Expresses love & respect

_____ Eats meals together

_____ Strong family relationships

_____ Productive arguments

_____ Quality time together

_____ Total divided by 10 = _____

Career

_____ Enjoy what I do

_____ Understand my job

_____ Good co-worker relationships

_____ Positive attitude and thoughts

_____ Stick to my schedule/plan

_____ Opportunity for advancement

_____ Keep track of my numbers

_____ Good planning & organizational skills

_____ Strong prospecting skills

_____ Productive

_____ Total divided by 10 = _____

Now, take the numbers you have from each of the Total lines and graph it on the following **Ideal Wheel** graph.

Ideal Wheel

Each of the "spokes" coming from the "hub" below respresents an "area" for achievement in your life. Rate your proficiency in each by placing an "X" through the number that best states where you are today. Then connect all your "X's" together. 1 is poor and 10 is excellent. This should give you a better outlook on the areas needing improvement.

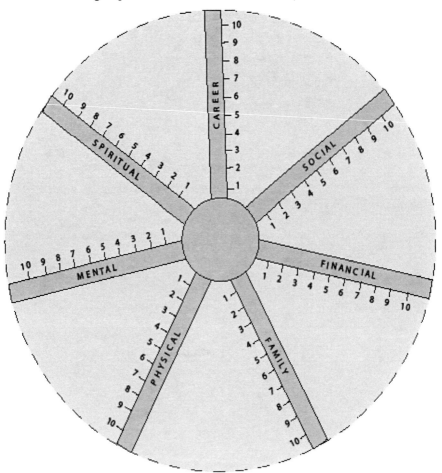

If your wheel is not perfectly round, as a car wheel is, your road to success in life will be "bumpy."

Next, draw a line connecting your scores to form a sort of circle. Some of your circles will look a bit off kilter. The goal is to have all tens and a perfectly rounded circle. But in reality, nobody does. However, when top producers connect their scores, their final image is more circle like than most people's. Top producers also seek to move towards the perfect circle each and every day.

The best way to gain balance in your life is to schedule EVERYTHING in your planner: business tasks, personal obligations, financial goals, etc. For example, if you're going to make Friday night date night with your significant other, then schedule it. If you're going to go to church or temple over the weekend, schedule it. If you're going to workout at the gym Monday morning, schedule it. If you're going to spend Saturday afternoon playing with your kids, schedule it. If you're going to go to the bank to set up a new retirement account, schedule it. Put your entire life in your planner.

Then, color code each activity. For example, you could use a yellow highlighter to indicate career tasks, a green one for personal, a blue one for financial, a pink one for physical, etc. Now you can do a quick glance of your weekly planner and see where you're missing some balance. So if all you see is yellow highlights and nothing else, you know you're neglecting a lot of other areas.

Additionally, establish some rules to live by. These rules can include such things as:

- I will only work late one night per week.

- I will workout three mornings a week.

- I will attend at least two of my children's activities each month.

- I will put ten percent of my paycheck towards my retirement account each week.

- I will go to church or temple at least twice per month.

- I will only work one weekend a month.

Determine what your rules to live by are and write them down. Make sure your spouse, children, and trusted co-workers or boss know your rules, too.

Finally, look at the **Ideal Wheel** regularly and refill it out on a regular basis to gauge where you are. After all, if you don't assess where you are, you can't improve.

Develop a PMA (Positive Mental Attitude)

Top producers have a positive mental attitude. Yes, we all know one or two top performers who are pains in the you know what. However, for the most part, top producers have a positive attitude. They don't let little things get them down. They have what I call a "Quick Bounce Back Factor."

Scott Robbins, an executive for Cyberhome Entertainment of Fremont, CA, a company that makes and distributes DVD players, says that you have to focus on what you can control, not what you can't. He explains that everyone experiences problems and challenges, and you will get down on yourself from time to time, but you have to bounce back quickly and focus on what you can control. When many people and many factors are involved, you sometimes have to just let things go and spend your time and energy on things that you can directly affect. He says that building relationships to a very strong level helps him deal better when problems arise. And building that relationship is something he controls.

I remember once when I got a large contract to help a physical education department raise money for a new weight room. I was so excited because they were going to be a $20,000 account (four times larger than my normal account). I was counting the commissions already, thinking about the big bonus check I was going to get.

I called them the night before to confirm everything. That's when I got the dreaded response: "Gary, I have been meaning to call you…"

Yes. I lost the account. I knew there was no value in moping around, so I put a positive twist on things and figured out a way to make lemonade out of lemons. What could I do to replace that $20,000? Since the large account was going to take most of the day to kick off (because of student presentations), if I didn't work with them I had the entire day to set appointments. So I got to work that evening and got my prospect lists together. The next day I got up early and started hammering away on the phone attempting to set ten appointments with groups that could do at least half of the $20,000. My goal was to set one appointment an hour over a course of ten hours. Because of my positive attitude, I actually set sixteen appointments. I was able to close ten of them for $88,000 in sales.

So I lost a $20,000 contract but picked up new ones totaling $88,000. Not too bad!

So much of a positive mental attitude deals with what you say when you talk to yourself. Unfortunately, we are wired to be hard on ourselves. We naturally want to say things like, "This is hard," or "I can't do this," when instead we should be saying positive things to ourselves, such as, "I can do this,' and "I'm good at this."

Often, before a phone call or a demo, I say to myself, "I can, I will, I'm going to." I've even been known to chant this line fifty to sixty times before a really important call. It is amazing how after you say this line repeatedly, you start to really get fired up and believe you are invincible.

Spencer Hays, one of the owners of the Southwestern Company, is one of the best salespeople I have ever met. He even has "sales professional" on his business card when he is actually a multi-million dollar executive. Spencer begins every morning by looking in the mirror and saying to himself, "I am happy, I am healthy, and I feel terrific." What a great way to start the day!

Take a moment now and create a couple of positive affirmations (Positive Self Talk) for yourself. Here are some examples to get your creative juices flowing:

- ◆ "I'm going to have the best day ever."

- ◆ "This is my next huge client."

- ◆ "I know I'm the best choice for this client."

- ◆ "I'm a lean, mean, selling machine."

Take some time to create a list of positive affirmations that would work for you. Keep the affirmation in the present tense, as in "I am" rather than the future tense, such as "I will be."

Once you create your affirmations, type them onto a sheet of paper, print it out, laminate it, punch a hole in the top corner, lace a plastic strand through the hole, and hang the affirmation sheet in your shower. This enables you to read your affirmations every day, first thing in the morning. Or you can post your affirmations up on your bathroom mirror. I write my affirmations on index cards and put them in my car: One in my visor, one taped to my dashboard, one taped to the corner of my window, etc. Then I read them while I'm sitting in traffic or at a red light. The key is to put these phrases in front of you as often as possible. That's the only way your mind will believe them and actually achieve them.

Hone Your Mindset for Success

If you invest in yourself, define your work ethic, get accountable, associate with successful people, strive for balance in life, and fill your mind with positive thoughts, you're going to make a major, positive change in your life. So what do you have to lose? Think about it...Whether you commit to developing the top producers mindset or not, time will still pass by. You can either wake up a month from now in the same spot you're at today, or you can wake up a month from now more successful and closer to your goals than ever before.

Additionally, top producers frequently tell me that they never have enough time in the day to accomplish everything they want. However, those who are average watch the clock continually and can't wait for the day to be over. So when you adopt the mindset of a top producer, your day will go quicker and you'll have a lot more fun. You'll make more money, get more done, and be happier in general.

So get ready to make some positive changes in your life right now. All it takes is a little planning, which we'll cover in the next chapter.

Notes

Chapter Three

The Value of Planning

If you are going to "get in," you must have a plan. But not just any old plan will do; to be successful, you must have a plan you are going to follow and not blow off, the way you blow off your dentist when you know you have a cavity! If you want to be truly successful and get in as many doors as possible, you must invest the time and energy to creating a plan that will work for you.

So what exactly is a "plan" in the sales profession? Having a plan means knowing what your final destination is and having the route planned of how to get there efficiently, one day at a time. Having a plan means knowing what you're doing hour by hour, all the while keeping your eye on the weeks and months. Having a plan means knowing how many hours each day you work, how many hours you prospect, how many dials you do, how many contacts you make, how many appointments you go on, how many presentations you do, and how many sales you close. All these details, when looked at closely, have to fit into what you do each day to get where you want to go.

After I graduated college, early in my sales career, I was one of the youngest salespeople on staff. Many people told me that I was too young or that I didn't have what it took to sell in the "real world." Well, when I heard that, I got inspired even more. I wanted to prove them wrong. So when my boss told me what it would take be successful, I took detailed notes and listened intently. I made out a plan and worked hard to make sure it became a reality. I put in extra hours at night and on the weekends. I studied my scripts. I connected with people and asked them to mentor me. I was determined not to fail.

Have you ever wanted something so bad that no matter what it took to get there you were willing to make the sacrifice? Do you remember how focused you were during that time? That's how you feel when you have a plan. What if you could have that feeling again?

If you've never felt that feeling, then I challenge you to answer this question: If I were to give you $5 million for simply putting together and enacting a plan to double what you generated in income last year, would you be able to come up with a plan? Would you really want to achieve it? How passionate and focused would you be? Well, if you really want to double your income next year, you need to dig deep and look for those feelings, as that's the only way you'll ever achieve any plan.

I recall a story that so clearly exhibits this point. Once upon a time there was a very successful businessman who had made millions of dollars through his business ventures. He lived in a small town where everyone knew everyone else. One day he was fishing out on the lake near his home, when a newcomer to town paddled his boat next to the successful man.

The newcomer said to the businessman: "Sir, everyone in town has told me that you are the most successful businessman around. You own several buildings and a fleet of cars, and if you don't own something in town, it's because you once did and then sold it. I must ask you, what is the key to your success?"

The businessman moved his boat next to the newcomer and beckoned the young man to come closer to him. The newcomer obliged. When he was inches from the businessman's face, the businessman pushed the newcomer into the water and held his head under the surface with all of his energy. The young man flailed his arms and did all he could to come to the top for air, but the businessman kept him under. Finally, the businessman let the newcomer up.

Huffing and puffing the newcomer yelled, "You crazy old man! Why did you do that to me?"

"Son, you asked me what it would take to be successful. Here is my answer. When you want success so bad—as bad as you wanted that breath of air you just got when I let you up—then you will be successful."

Plan Your Way to Success

Since you are reading this book, you definitely want to be successful. But in order to be successful, you have to know what success means *to you*. Does it mean making a certain amount of money? Does it mean being in the top

10% of your company or industry? Does it mean being healthy and at your goal weight, thereby feeling better about yourself? Does it mean knowing that you are financially secure and have all your bills and retirement plans under control? Whatever success means to you, define it and internalize it.

As the old man in my previous story taught us, you have to really want success. When you really want it, things will begin to become easy to achieve. If you're not 100% sure of what you want or even why you want it, then things are difficult. Why? Because when you know what you want, you're more attuned to what you need, and you notice opportunities you may have otherwise overlooked. Additionally, you're now more motivated to actually do what you need to do, because you want something so bad that failure is no longer an option. Realize, though, that in order to make a significant change in your life, the pain of staying the same has to be bigger than the pain of change—only then will you truly take action.

The good news is that planning is relatively simple. In fact, there are only four things you can put in your plan that will change your current circumstance:

1. You can plan to do more of a certain thing.

2. You can plan to do less of a certain thing.

3. You can plan to start doing things that you are not doing now. In other words, you can change your focus.

4. You can plan to stop doing certain things all together.

Sometimes, if you're making a big change, you may need to plan to do all four of these things to get the results you desire. Let me give you a personal example. Recently, I wanted to lose some fat and build muscle. You know how it is: When you get older your body doesn't react like it used to and fat jumps onto your body the way a lion pounces on its prey. When you were in your teens and twenties you could eat a whole bag of potato chips and nothing would happen. But when you are in your forties, you eat just one chip and the Bs expand (the belly and butt).

In my case, it wasn't about how much I weighed; it was about how I looked and fit into my clothing. It was also about some commitments I had made to certain people, and my word means a lot to me. So I made the following plan:

Do more of:

- ❑ I will do more cardio (two to six days per week).

- ❑ I will increase my water consumption from 1.5 liters to at least 3 liters per day.

Do less of:

- ❑ I will eat less bread and non-healthy types of snack foods, as well as cut back on the diet soft drinks.

Start doing:

- ❑ I will start eating every three hours a balanced meal of 40% protein and carbohydrates and 20% fat.

- ❑ I will write down everything I ate in a journal. I then have to share this journal with my weight trainer or else I have to pay him $20 every time I show up to train without it.

Stop doing:

- ❑ I will stop making excuses why I can't get my run in or can't make it to the gym to work out. Being too cold, too busy, or too tired are no longer acceptable. And I believe it is easier to stop making excuses because I have put all of the other activities in place.

No matter what you want to change, whether it's losing weight, prospecting more, asking for referrals, etc., these four steps used in combination with each other will be what sets you a part from all those who never reach their dreams. For example, here's what your list might looks like if you're goal was to prospect more.

Do more of:

❏ I will do more phone time. I will schedule it in daily when I plan my week, and I won't fall below fifteen hours per week of scheduled phone time.

Do less of:

❏ I will do less talking and more listening. I will remember the phrase: "God gave me two ears and one mouth for a reason."

Start doing:

❏ I will be more creative with my marketing ideas. I will be different than the rest of my competition.

Stop doing:

❏ I will stop making excuses for not putting in enough prospecting hours.

Now it's time to begin your plan. Answer the following questions:

❏ What one thing do you want to change in your personal life? (Write it down)

❏ What one thing do you want to change in your professional life? (Write it down)

Use the following goal sheet to help you fine tune your plan.

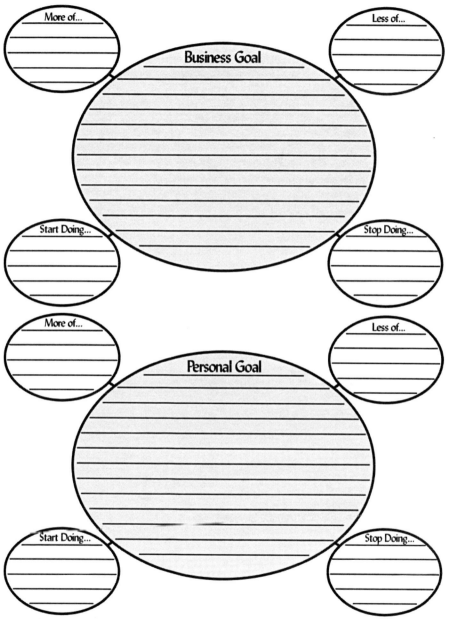

Fill in each of the blanks indicated so you can identify what you need to do more off, less of, start doing, or stop doing. Then, give the sheet to your mentor, significant other, or whoever is holding you accountable for your goals. Also, laminate a copy and keep it with you so you can review it often.

Why Plan?

Planning helps you increase your "return on your energy." Think of it this way: For every minute you spend planning your activities, goals, time, etc., you save, on average, ten minutes on the work it involves in executing these plans.

To determine how much time you should devote to planning, use this formula:

Number of minutes allocated for the activity divided by ten equals the amount of time you should devote to planning.

So, assuming you put in an eight hour day in the field (480 minutes), you need to put in at least forty-eight minutes in planning to have an effectively planned day (480 divided by 10 = 48).

I highly recommend that you do this planning the night before, because you'll sleep much better and will be a more relaxed person all evening when you know your plan for the following day.

The key to being a good planner is to have a good personal calendar and scheduling system. Any system will work from the Franklin Planner, to a Palm Pilot, to a Blackberry, to Microsoft Outlook. Whatever system you decide to use, list every goal, task, idea, contact name, and responsibility in your system. Here is an example from my daily planner.

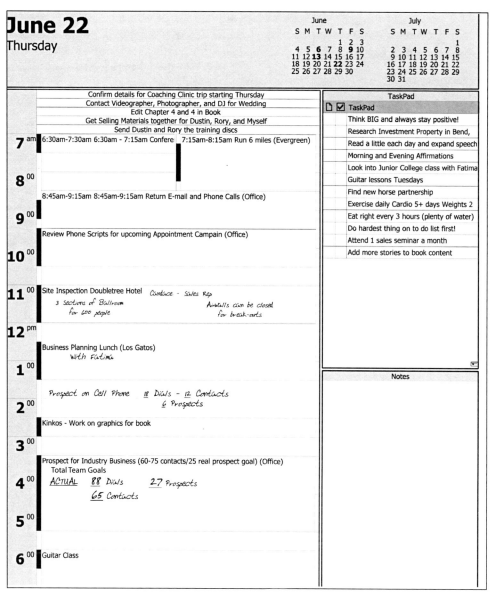

June 22
Thursday

June
S	M	T	W	T	F	S
				1	2	3
4	5	**6**	7	8	**9**	10
11	12	**13**	14	15	16	17
18	19	20	21	**22**	23	24
25	26	27	28	29	30	

July
S	M	T	W	T	F	S
						1
2	3	4	5	6	7	8
9	10	11	12	13	14	15
16	17	18	19	20	21	22
23	24	25	26	27	28	29
30	31					

Confirm details for Coaching Clinic trip starting Thursday
Contact Videographer, Photographer, and DJ for Wedding
Edit Chapter 4 and 4 in Book
Get Selling Materials together for Dustin, Rory, and Myself
Send Dustin and Rory the training discs

7 am 6:30am-7:30am 6:30am - 7:15am Confere   7:15am-8:15am Run 6 miles (Evergreen)

8 00

8:45am-9:15am 8:45am-9:15am Return E-mail and Phone Calls (Office)

9 00

Review Phone Scripts for upcoming Appointment Campain (Office)

10 00

11 00 Site Inspection Doubletree Hotel   *Candace - Sales Rep*
   3 sections of Ballroom   *Airwalls can be closed*
   for 600 people   *for break-outs*

12 pm

Business Planning Lunch (Los Gatos)
   With Fatima

1 00

   Prospect on Cell Phone   18 Dials - 12 Contacts
                            6 Prospects

2 00

Kinkos - Work on graphics for book

3 00

Prospect for Industry Business (60-75 contacts/25 real prospect goal) (Office)
   Total Team Goals

4 00 *ACTUAL   88 Dials   27 Prospects*
            65 Contacts

5 00

6 00 Guitar Class

TaskPad

☐ ☑ TaskPad

Think BIG and always stay positive!
Research Investment Property in Bend,
Read a little each day and expand speech
Morning and Evening Affirmations
Look into Junior College class with Fatima
Guitar lessons Tuesdays
Find new horse partnership
Exercise daily Cardio 5+ days Weights 2
Eat right every 3 hours (plenty of water)
Do hardest thing on to do list first!
Attend 1 sales seminar a month
Add more stories to book content

Notes

When you plan, be sure to only plan one day at a time. Why? Well, if you're like most people, you can plan a single day quicker and easier than planning an entire week, month, or year. Of course you want to look at the entire week and month in terms of time efficiency and scheduling, but make the most important focus on planning several great days, one day at a time. Then, when you have several good days and put them together, you will have several good weeks, good months, and even good years.

To make the most of your days, consider using a quadrant planning system, where you break your territory up into four quadrants, **A-B-C-D**. I have used such a system for years and it works great. Here's how you do it: All **A** prospects are located on the northwest side of town, for example, all **B** prospect are on the northeast side of town, all **C** prospects are on the southwest side of town, and all **D** prospects are on the southeast side of town. I then put these little letters on my calendar, so that Monday is an **A** day, for example, Tuesday is a **B** day, Wednesday is a **C** day, and Thursday is a **D** day. Then, when I am attempting to set an appointment I can say, "I will be in your area on this day and this day."

Additionally, since I spend so much time in the car, it has also helped me to have at least ten good leads and contacts whom I want to reach while I drive. You can use this time for flat out prospecting, or you can use it to follow up and service the clients you already have. When I started taking the time to have these ten names and numbers, my production went up. In fact, I had my best three years at Great American Opportunities when I started doing this. Also, it definitely helps to have an ear piece for your cell phone so you don't have to hold the phone while driving. Additionally, in some states driving while holding a cell phone is illegal, so an ear piece is a must.

Here are some more planning keys that will enable you to plan more effectively.

10 Keys to Proper Planning

1. <u>Your daily schedule should be something everyone knows about and can see</u>. That's everyone—your boss, your co-workers, your significant other, etc. You want other people to know what you're planning to do so they can hold you accountable to your plan. I have a white board up in my office with my daily goals and schedule listed. I have seen people much more fanatical than me actually print out their calendar and give it to several of their peers in the office.

2. <u>For twenty-one days, keep an hour-by-hour schedule of exactly what you are doing.</u> Share this with your boss or a peer you greatly respect. Look for areas in which you are being most productive and see where you are wasting the most time. Be honest! At the end of the twenty-one days, add up how many hours you spent doing each of the following activities:

- ❐ Driving

- ❐ Planning

- ❐ Paperwork

- ❐ Other administrative duties

- ❐ Eating meals alone or with clients

- ❐ Spending time with co-workers

- ❐ Spending time in meetings

- ❐ Thinking

- ❐ Writing letters, thank you notes, and e-mails

- ❐ Waiting on hold or for an appointment

- ❐ Appointment setting

- ❐ Presenting your product

- ❐ Prospecting

- ❐ Anything else you do on a regular basis

I have included a Time Awareness Log to help you keep track of your day. Photocopy the following sheet and use it to keep track of your activities each day.

TIME AWARENESS LOG

Name: _____ Date: _____

Start & Stop Times	Activity and Description. Be Specific!

Review your time logs every evening and you'll quickly notice a pattern to how you spend your time. Often, you'll be amazed at your findings. I know that every time I fill out this sheet, I find that I spend too much time in my car and not enough time prospecting and setting appointments. Knowing this information

57

motivates me to tighten up my appointments so that I am not going back and forth across town so often.

3. **Identify your daily priorities.** The 21 day exercise previously discussed will help you clarify what your priorities are. For most of us in sales, our priorities are prospecting, paperwork, follow up, presenting, and planning. By identifying what your priorities are, you will plan your day accordingly so you don't neglect the most important aspects to your success.

   You have probably heard of the Franklin Covey Planning System, which uses an **A-B-C** system. Your **A** tasks are your MUST DO items. Your **B** tasks are your SHOULD DO items. And your **C** tasks are your DO IT IF YOU HAVE TIME items. Several similar systems are available, and they all focus on prioritizing tasks. I have used such a system for years, and it helps me get my priorities straight.

Identify below what your main priorities are every day.

_____
_____
_____
_____

4. **No errands or trivial work during the critical eight to ten hours of work time, at least four of the five work days.** I know this sounds very rigid, but this practice alone can help you improve your time management. I get my gas, pick up my dry cleaning, go to the post office, go to the bank, and work out all before 7:30 a.m. or after 5:00 p.m. if at all possible. If you must do any trivial work or errands during the day, make sure you only do them one day a week. This one practice will help keep you on track and focused.

5. **Know your numbers.** How many contacts does it take for you to get one appointment? How many appointments does it take for you to get one presentation? How many presentations does it take for you to get one sale? The only way to know your numbers is to keep track of them.

Here is a sample scorekeeping sheet that will help you keep track of your progress.

DATE: _____	**TIME ON PHONE:** _____
APPOINTMENT GOAL: _____	**DIAL GOAL:** _____
CONTACT GOAL: _____	**REFERRAL GOAL:** _____

DIALS:

_____

MESSAGES LEFT: (100 Minimum – 12 per hour Goal)

_____

Names of Contacts for APPOINTMENTS

Name	Date & Time	Name	Date & Time
1 _____		6 _____	
2 _____		7 _____	
3 _____		8 _____	
4 _____		9 _____	
5 _____		10 _____	

Names of Contacts NOT INTERESTED:

1 _____		6 _____	
2 _____		7 _____	
3 _____		8 _____	
4 _____		9 _____	
5 _____		10 _____	

Names of REFERRALS:

1 _____		6 _____	
2 _____		7 _____	
3 _____		8 _____	
4 _____		9 _____	
5 _____		10 _____	

You will need to keep track of your numbers for at least a month, sometimes longer, to get a clear idea of the exact number of activities you need to get results. After you determine your numbers, talk to some of the top producers in your company or industry to find out their numbers and how yours compare.

I recently spent the day traveling with Gary Cruff of Ameriprise Financial Services in Campbell, California. Gary knew his numbers. One of his biggest prospecting techniques is to have people leave their business card in a fish bowl at two local restaurants in hopes of winning a free lunch for themselves and seven other people. Gary buys the lunch and takes ten minutes to casually introduce himself and the services he provides to the eight people attending. Each time he leaves one of these fish bowls he knows that:

❐ He will collect twenty business cards per week per restaurant.

❐ Ten of the twenty people will be legitimate prospects he finds worthwhile to call based on profession.

❐ Four of the ten people he speaks with will accept the lunch.

❐ Two of the four people will end up attending the lunch.

❐ He does four lunches per week on two different days back to back (11:30 a.m. and 1:30 p.m.).

❐ Usually all eight invitees attend.

❐ Six out of the eight are interested in more information.

❐ But only one new client results from every lunch.

❐ Lunch costs $12 a head, for a total of $200 for two lunches that day.

❐ Each new client Gary picks up equals approximately $1,200 per year in income.

❐ More than half of his clients will be with him for longer than ten years, and every year he earns an average of $1,200 per client. Over a span of ten years, that's a lifetime value of $12,000 per person.

By Gary knowing his numbers he is able to determine a couple of things. First, he may be able to do a little better job of selling the benefits in his ten minutes so that he can get a better ratio of people buying his services. Second, he knows he needs to hire help in order to do more luncheons so that others can duplicate this process.

6. <u>Think of your schedule like a high school class schedule</u>. In high school, when the bell rang at the end of class, you automatically moved from one subject to the next. You never questioned or second guessed the schedule; you just moved on and did what you were supposed to do. Likewise, your schedule today should be like a well-oiled machine. Do not compromise what needs to get done. If you stick to your schedule every day (i.e.: Prospect from 8:00 a.m. to 11:00 a.m., Present from 11:30 a.m. to 2:30 p.m., and Follow Up and Do Paperwork from 3:00 p.m. to 6:00 p.m.), you will always have time the next day to finish up what you didn't finish today. Of course, there will always be exceptions to this, but if you follow this philosophy as often as possible, you will definitely get more done.

7. <u>Know what every minute and hour is worth to you</u>. For example, let's say you earn $100,000 a year, you work forty-eight weeks a year (two weeks vacation and two weeks of personal time), and you work forty hours a week. That means you earn $52.08 an hour or .87 a minute. Knowing this information will certainly keep you from wasting time. Now you won't drive across town for an appointment unless you have confirmed it and pre-qualified the prospect. Why? Because if that trip and prep time took you three hours, and the prospect was not in for some reason, you just lost $156.24. On top of that, you also lost the opportunity to use that time on a qualified prospect that may have earned you a lot more than the $156. People always tell me that they want to be worth $100 an hour, yet they waste so much time each day. If you knew you were making $100 an hour, would wasting an hour a day, five hours a week, twenty hours a month, or $2,000 a month bother you? That is $24,000 a year!

Figure out below what you are worth every hour and minute. Refer back to my example as a guide to help you figure out these numbers.

> Each hour I am worth $ _____.
>
> Each minute I am worth $ _____.

8. <u>**Don't be overly attached to the results.**</u> Be focused on the activity that will produce the results. Too often people get so down on themselves if they have a slump. But if you know that it takes a certain number of calls to get a certain number of appointments and deals, then you won't stress so much because of the "law of averages." You also always have the ability to tape record yourself, have somebody watch you and give feedback, or get additional training if your numbers drop. But once you know what it takes to be successful, never compromise on the activity.

9. <u>**Accept rejection with professionalism and deal with it.**</u> Remember the phrase, "Some will, some won't, so what! Next!"

   If you know that you have other prospects to see, you will not care if you get a "no." In most cases the prospect is not rejecting you; he or she is rejecting what you have to offer. I've always thought of rejection like this: If someone rejects me, "no" means "next."

   Always leave the prospect with a good taste in his or her mouth, because if you cannot position yourself as the number one vendor, then you better position yourself as the number two choice. This is so important, because when clients change (and they will) they will not be calling their third or fourth choice. They will be calling their second choice. Make that you.

   For years I have mentally referred to my "picket fence example" to put me at ease about how rejection worked. I have also shared this thought with several others, and everybody seems to get a lot from it.

Picket Fence Example

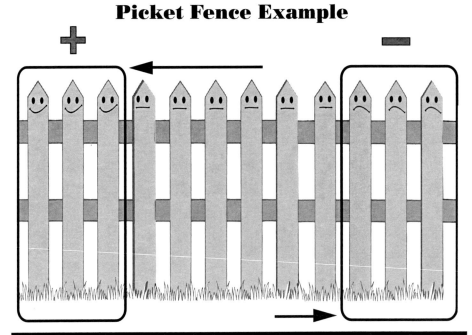

How many of these middle pickets can we get to the positive side?

- Each picket equals 1 prospect.

- In this example, 12 contacts a day is good for this sales rep.

- In this example, industry standard was 25% of people called on were positive and 25% of people were negative.

- Your industry or career may be different. What are your percentages?

- Verbiage, tone of voice, appearance, use of a third party name in the approach, & polished presentation skills are just a few things you can do to get the middle pickets to the positive side.

- Understanding that you will always have a certain percentage of your prospects negative and positive will allow you to focus on the middle group, and not focus on the rejection you receive from negative people.

You will notice the circle around the three pickets to the right and left to the diagram. You will also notice a + sign above the left pickets, meaning a POSITIVE response, and a – sign above the pickets to the right, meaning a NEGATIVE response. You will also notice that with the remaining six pickets in the middle there is an arrow above four of them pointing in the positive direction, and an arrow below two of the middle pickets pointing in the negative direction.

What does all of this mean? Out of every twelve people I talk to, I expect three to be very positive. They will say things such as, "I'm glad you called." Or, "Yes. Let's set up an appointment." I also expect three to be negative. They may rip into me, my company, or whatever they can rip into. I am not bothered by these three because I expect them and plan for them.

The middle six pickets are the most important, because your sales skills and techniques will be the difference between getting them to go right (negative) or left (positive). What and how you say things on the phone or in person will determine which way they go. Do you use third party? Do you sound polished? Are you assumptive? Are you talking with them or at them?

If you are prepared to get rejection, even expect it, then you can focus all of your energy on the positive people you want to work with. To prepare, answer the following questions:

❏ How many calls and contacts per day do I typically make?

❏ How many pickets are positive and negative for me?

❏ What do I currently do to middle pickets to get them to the positive side?

❏ What can I do differently with my middle pickets to get them closer to the positive side?

10. **If you don't have an assistant or a plan of what it will take to get one, then you are an assistant earning an assistant's pay.** Don't do the $5 an hour jobs. Having an assistant to help you get the little things done is a huge benefit to you. Even having a partner,

if he or she is good, is worth the money you have to invest. Why? Because there are only so many hours in a day to get things done and only so many ways you can look at a particular situation. I have always felt that I would rather have a smaller piece of a big pie than a bigger piece of a small pie. Yes, it will cost you some money to get good help, but if you use that help correctly, they will pay for themselves ten times over, and then some. I have had assistants over the years to prospect, service my accounts, do all the mailings, run errands, manage the website, create marketing pieces, etc.

Here are some tips for working with an assistant:

- ❏ Know exactly how many sales you need to get and maintain an assistant. Also have a goal of the level of sales you would need to hit to get a second assistant.

- ❏ If you have an assistant, you must be willing to let go and delegate.

- ❏ Set up a daily or weekly meeting with your assistant to go over the "to do" list, concerns, changes, etc. Give your assistant permission to solve problems and be proactive. Empower your assistant.

- ❏ Take your time in the hiring process. I have had a lot of success with Craig's List and will often look at several resumes and speak with several candidates before limiting it down to the five I will interview. And of course, get a referral from someone you know as opposed to placing an ad.

- ❏ Don't hire someone because he or she is "just like you" or because the person looks a certain way. Hire someone for what he or she will produce. Check the person's references. I went through a phase where I hired assistants who "looked the part." But none of them were worth the salary I paid. When I put aside my image of what an assistant should look like and hired based on skills and productivity, I found an assistant who stayed with me for over ten years and who contributed enormously to my success.

❏ Train your assistant well. Take your assistant on ride-alongs so he or she can understand the job.

❏ Share your goals and objectives with your staff, as it makes them feel a part of something big and lets them know they have a position of importance. The term "assistant" doesn't imply menial jobs either. The CEO is, in effect, an assistant to the Board of Directors. And the Vice President of the United States is an assistant to the President. Assistants are very important because they ease our burden so we can get more done.

❏ Praise and acknowledgement are important, as are one-minute reprimands when they slip up.

❏ Pay fair market value plus five to ten percent if you want to maintain quality people. I like to give my staff bonuses based on if I hit my sales goal or not. Also, I'm a big believer in a yearly ten percent raise if the person is reliable.

A lot of people also invest in a house cleaning service and gardener because the time you spend doing those tasks could have been much better spent on your business or with your family.

What's Your Plan?

During my travels with different sales reps from different industries, I posed this question to them: "What separates the top producers from average producers?" Almost every one of them answered as follows: "The top producers are great planners. They use their time efficiently. They know where they want to go and they have a plan to get there." That's powerful stuff!

If you want to double your income within a year, then you need to begin planning. If you currently do not plan, then I challenge you to begin today. If you currently are planning, then I challenge you to look at the ten keys I just gave you and pick out two or three you can really improve on. Work diligently on the keys that challenge you, and you'll soon have a foolproof plan that will propel you to the top.

Remember the old adage: "If you fail to plan, you plan to fail."

Notes

Chapter Four

Set Your Goals

B y now you're likely thinking, "I'm excited about all the changes I want to make, but like New Year's Resolutions that I said I would stick to, all my changes often become unstuck. What can I do to make them stick?"

Here is when some good goal setting comes into play.

Most salespeople are naturally very goal-oriented. For example, if you are very motivated to win a trip, then you'll do whatever it takes to get it, including working extra hours and planning your route. You have the goal of winning the trip and you do what you must to reach that goal. Unfortunately, that's often where the goals end. Unless there's some "prize" at the end, like a trip or an award, many salespeople neglect to make goals for themselves. Why? Because they often have a "back up" for themselves. Here's what I mean.

Let's say you want to earn $200,000 this year. Based on your sales commission structure, that means you would have to make four hundred sales for the year, if you made $500 per sale, on average. But if you only made three hundred sales, which earned you $150,000, you'd be okay because you have the other $50,000 available on your home equity line of credit. Because you have that "safety net," you don't strive for your goals as much as you would if you didn't have that home equity available to you.

Realize that most people are motivated by pain rather than pleasure. That means they're more apt to do something that keeps them out of harm's way than they are to do something that brings them a prize. So if you don't have any equity in your house and you need money, you're going to sell and make the money you need. But if it's too easy to refinance and pull money out of your house, you won't work as hard to reach your sales goals.

To help you with effective goal setting, follow these five keys:

1. **Quantify what you want.** Don't be vague. For example, don't say you want to sell more products. Be specific about how much you want to sell. For example, you could say, "This year my goal is to sell 50% more products than I did last year."

2. **Set a deadline for your goal, and break your goal down into smaller pieces.** Without a self-imposed pressure point to this commitment, you will quickly postpone your intended change. For example, with a sales goal, if your goal is to sell twenty-five of your highest ticket products in six months, that is approximately four products a month, or one product a week. If you know your numbers and know that you need to make fifty contacts to sell one product, you now know exactly how many people you must contact each week to reach your goal. This goal is now a lot more manageable.

3. **Change only one or two things at a time.** If your goal involves change, don't try to change everything at once. People generally don't like change in the first place, so really focus on one or two things you want to accomplish. Once you're successful with those, then move onto the next thing.

4. **Be realistic.** You can only accomplish a certain amount of things in a certain period of time. Set goals that are attainable. For example, if you say you're going to prospect five thousand people a day, that's simply not possible, and you're setting yourself up for failure. However, if you say you're going to prospect one hundred people a day, that may be realistic, depending on your industry. As you begin to better know your limits and boundaries, you can increase your goals.

5. **Put your goals in writing.** You will not be able to effectively accomplish your goals unless you write them down and review them often. In fact, Harvard University did a study on goals, and here are their findings:

- 27% of the people studied had given no thought to goals at all.

- 60% of the people studied had given a little thought to their goals, but they were mostly about financial goals.

- 10% of the people studied had a good idea of what they wanted in life, but nothing written down.

- 3% had concrete written goals that they reviewed regularly.

Of the same people studied

- 60% were living in modest means.

- 27% were barely existing.

- 10% were moderately successful.

- 3% were highly successful.

Of the 3% and 10%, both had the same education, but the 3% had reduced their goals down to writing, and the 10% had not. As a result, the 3% out-performed the rest of the people ten to one, or more! That proves the power of committing your goals to writing.

Use Your Goals to Help You Succeed

Simply having some goals is one thing; now you must use your goals to propel you to success. But how? How do you strive to achieve all your goals without burning out?

One of the simplest ways to make goal attainment easier is to break your day up into three distinct goal accomplishment periods. For example, your three time periods can be 8:00 a.m. to 11:00 a.m., 11:30 a.m. to 2:30 p.m., and 3:00 p.m. to 6:00 p.m. Then rather than try to prospect one hundred people in a day, your goal is to prospect thirty-three people during each time window.

I learned this technique when I sold books. Since our daily goal was to give thirty demos, it was a much more doable goal if I broke it up as doing ten demos in the first part of the day, ten in the middle, and the final ten in the final few hours. We even had 3" x 5" index cards that we used to keep track of where we were each goal period.

Remember, you'll always find it much easier to reach your targets when you break things down into smaller chunks.

Another technique to ensure you reach your goals is to make a game of always staying a certain number of appointments ahead of yourself (or a certain number of steps ahead needed to accomplish your goal). For example, how many appointments ahead would make you feel comfortable? For me in the fundraising business, it was always to stay at least ten appointments ahead. When I was doing some of my network marketing businesses, it was always to stay at least three ahead.

By doing this, you'll sell much differently. You won't sell with a sense of pressure, nor will you push so much. You'll feel so much more confident when you can go into your demo and say to your prospects: "Let me go ahead and show you what I do. If you like it, then we can set something up to work together. If you don't like it, that is okay too, because I have nine other people like you who I'll be showing this to this week. So there is no pressure here. If it works, it works. If not, then maybe we can work together in the future and still be friends." (I even like to show my full calendar to the prospect here so he or she can see that I really do have a lot of other people lined up.)

Keep Track of Your Goals

One of the best ways to keep track of all your goals is to have a Goals Notebook. This notebook is actually a binder that you can add and remove pages from easily. In my notebook I keep track of the following:

1. My **Ideal Wheel.**

2. Ten goals to accomplish that year (personal and professional).

3. My dream list and timeline.

4. Pictures of things I would like to purchase and places I would like to go.

5. Goal charts that I am currently following the progress of.

6. Motivational quotes and stories.

7. Notes from good books I have read.

I schedule one hour every week to review this notebook and make changes. I usually do this Sunday night or Monday morning, as it is a great way to start the week. I also carry the notebook with me. Then, whenever I have an extra few minutes, I can pull it out and review it.

If you're the technological type of person who doesn't like "old fashioned" notebooks and binders, you can keep track of all this on your computer. I'm the type of person who likes to actually see, touch, and feel things, so for me, a computer screen of my goals, plans, and motivational messages wouldn't be enough, but for you it may work quite well.

Whether you're using a notebook or a computer file, each year you update your goals and any other pages. While some people may think keeping track of all this is silly, realize that when you review something every day, it becomes a part of who you are. By now we've all heard the expression "Out of sight, out of mind." That message applies to your goals too.

I once heard someone say, "You become what you think about, so think about your goals daily and they will become a reality." Your goals notebook helps you do precisely that.

Make Your Goals a Reality Today

During my twenty-one years in the sales profession, I have noticed that those salespeople with goals were always the ones up on stage winning awards, going on company trips, receiving large paychecks, and driving the nicest cars. Those with no concrete goals didn't win trips, didn't get the big paychecks, and didn't last long in the business,

On which side of the spectrum would you rather be? Would you rather be winning the awards and earning the big money, or would you rather be struggling every month to pay your bills and hopping from one sales job to the next? I think the answer is obvious. You want to win BIG! Well, to do so, you need some goals. So I challenge you to come up with a minimum of three business related goals for yourself today, and then create your plan to reaching those goals. By doing so, you'll be one step closer to getting in more sales doors and getting out with new business.

Notes

Chapter Five

The Facts
on Prospecting

In order to "get in" with anyone, you must have prospected them in some way. Maybe you called a referral someone you work with gave you. Maybe you cold-called a decision maker. Maybe you sent an e-mail to a qualified buyer. Maybe you even paid someone else to prospect for you, such as a telemarketer or office assistant. Regardless of the way you prospected someone, the bottom line is that unless you get the appointment, anything else I can share with you would be wasted. That's why we're going to spend a good bit of time on the concept of prospecting, as well as the various ways you could prospect someone successfully.

I know, I know…you've likely already read many sales books and attended seminars on what to do when you get in front of your prospect. But the real question is, how do you get in to see the prospect? Until you get in, what you say, how you look, and what you present are irrelevant.

I have done extensive research on prospecting over the years. And I have found that, on average, prospecting accounts for forty-five percent of a successful salesperson's time, energy, and talent. Here's the exact breakdown of what they do the other fifty-five percent of the time:

- ◆ Twenty percent of people's time is spent on developing presentation skills and meeting with prospects and clients.

- ◆ Another twenty percent of people's time is spent continually learning all they can about their service, product, and industry.

♦ And the last fifteen percent of the work week of successful salespeople's time is spent in personal and professional development, including reading, listening to CDs, and exercising.

You can view prospecting, like anything else in life, as either positive or negative. If you think of prospecting positively, as something that will bring you pleasure, you will plant the seeds of success. However, if you think of it negatively, you choose to focus on the rejection involved in prospecting and possibly the time it takes to actually do it. If you hate prospecting and cold calling, when you have to do it, the phone feels like it weighs a thousand pounds. These people subconsciously get so scared of rejection that it paralyzes them and prevents them from succeeding.

The Six Prospecting Challenges

In order to NOT fear prospecting, you have to understand why it is difficult for you. In general, there are six main reasons why people have a problem with prospecting. If you can understand your difficult part and then put a plan in place to conquer the fear, then you'll no longer view prospecting as a bad thing. And if you currently have a positive outlook on prospecting and can focus on getting better in these six areas, then you will make more money in the long run.

Challenge #1: I don't know how to prospect.

Ignorance is not bliss, especially when it comes to prospecting. If you truly don't know how to prospect, then keep reading, not only this book, but also other sales books that can give you insights. Also, listen to training CDs, talk with top producers, do role playing with your manager and other top producers engage in any other activity that will give you the prospecting information you need. In today's information age, not knowing something is no longer an excuse.

Challenge #2: I have unproductive work habits.

When you're unproductive during the day, in most cases, it's because you don't have enough motivation to stay focused. You can't see the value in starting early and working late. Very often your poor work habits come from poor training you may have received. To develop the productive work habits you need to succeed at prospecting, seek out the successful people in your field. Learn what they are doing and imitate that.

For example, when I was at Great American Opportunities, I worked with a gentleman who was doing about average year after year. Although I was not his direct manager, I had an opportunity to travel with him and almost serve as a mentor to him. What I found out shocked me. He was a single dad and had to drop off his kids at school in the morning. As a result, he wasn't able to start work in the morning until about 9:30 a.m. At around 3:00 p.m. he had to pick up his children from school and bring them to the daycare. At the end of the day, he had to pick up the kids by 6:00 p.m., which meant he had to stop working at 5:15 p.m.

When I analyzed the situation, I found that he only had, on average, about five hours worth of prospecting time each day. We had an in-depth conversation about this. We deduced that for him to reach the level of sales success he wanted, he needed to put in a solid eight hour day.

So I challenged him to find a daycare facility that would do the following:

◆ Allow him to drop the kids off before school

◆ Transport the kids to school at the appropriate time

◆ Pick the kids up after school

He spent about an hour on the phone until he found a daycare facility that would do this. Even better, this facility was actually $100 per month cheaper than the place he had been using.

The following year, his sales doubled...all because he changed one unproductive habit!

Challenge #3: I don't know what to say when prospecting.
In the next few chapters we will spend a good deal of time going over the exact verbiage to use when prospecting. Your job is to actually practice these scripts and then use them when you prospect.

Challenge #4: I have a difficult time handling rejection and get embarrassed quite easily.
If this is your challenge, then you must make a decision today: Either you totally muscle up and decide that you are going to get over this fear, or you give in to your fear and always attain mediocre results. Remember that the more you do the thing you fear, the better you get at it. A simple example is

running your hand over a burning candle. After you do it once, you can get a little closer the next time as you learn the area in which you burn yourself.

FEAR is really an acronym for False Evidence Appearing Real. And usually, the thing we fear the most never actually happens. Dave Dean, author of the book *Now is Your Time to Win*, says we need to be willing to fail if we are going to grow. He says that the failure to face fear never resolves it; it only gives it time to grow.

By now, most people know that the definition of "insanity" is "doing the same thing over and over and expecting a different result." But do you know what the definition of "futility" is? It's knowing the definition of "insanity" and still not doing anything about it.

What are you doing over and over, knowing full well that you'll get the same old results, but are too afraid to change? If you don't have it in you to muscle up and get over your fear, then you need to be prepared to reach for your wallet and hire a professional telemarketing company to prospect for you.

Challenge #5: No one is holding me accountable.

People ask me all the time, "Who should I get to keep me accountable?" I usually reply with one of two answers. First, if you have a good boss who you totally respect and who has a motivational aspect to him or her, then that person would be one choice. Simply ask your boss to hold you accountable. If you can, set up some sort of strict rewards and consequences program. If you don't have a strong support system from your boss, or if you have a strong boss but feel you need more, then the second choice is to hire a sales coach. Since you are paying this person, you obviously want to grow and will do what he or she recommends. A coach will definitely hold you accountable and teach you things that will pay for the coaching ten times over, and in some cases a lot more than that.

Challenge #6: I don't keep track of my numbers and results.

If I called you right now, and if you were at the top of your game, you should be able to tell me the following:

- How many contacts you must make each day to hit your goal

- How many contact you must make to get one appointment

♦   How many appointments you must make to get one contract

♦   Your closing percentage

♦   Your average sales amount

If you had to fill these items in on some sort of report, even if you showed it to nobody, you would at least have a target to shoot for. So many salespeople are wandering generalities, not knowing what they want or where they are going! In a previous chapter I gave you a sheet to track your numbers. Use it!

The Positive Side of Prospecting

Now that you know what may be challenging you when it comes to prospecting, let's look at the positive side of prospecting.

Realize that prospecting allows you to turn a pile of leads into a pile of money through the effective use of the telephone or yourself in person. In other words, the more you prospect, the more money you make. And the more money you make usually means you are less stressed. Granted, this is not always true, but if you are ahead in your numbers and are making the amount of money you need to live a comfortable lifestyle, then you tend to be a bit happier.

In fact, if you knew what a dial was worth to you and knew your specific goals, you would probably be more motivated to prospect.

Let me give you an example of this from my past job of fundraising. The following were my actual numbers:

Dials: <u>100</u>

Contacts: <u>30</u>

Appointments: <u>10</u>

Demonstrations: <u>9</u> (one would often cancel)

Contracts for Sale: <u>4</u>

Average Sale: <u>$8,000</u>

Total Sales as a Result of Dials: <u>$32,000</u>

Commission: <u>20%</u>

Actual Commission ($32,000 x 20%) as a Result of Dials: $6,400

Total Sales for Every Dial: $320

Total Commission for Every Dial: $64

That means for every 100 dials I made, I would make 30 contacts. From those 30 contacts, I'd get 10 appointments. From those 10 appointments, I'd make 9 demonstrations. From those 9 demonstrations, I'd get 4 sales. Since each sale was worth approximately $8,000, that would equal $32,000 in new business. My commission was 20% of the sale, meaning I'd earn $6,400 from those 4 sales. Since I made 100 dials, each dial was worth $320 in sales and $64 in commission. That meant each time I picked up the phone, I was putting $64 in my pocket. Ch-ching!

If you knew exactly what every dial meant to you, would you be more motivated to make the dial? I think so!

So assuming doing the prospecting took you fifteen to twenty hours a week, and you worked forty to fifty hours a week, doesn't it make sense to do the prospecting every week, no matter what? Even if you are too busy to prospect, you can hire a telemarketing company to do it for you, or you can hire an assistant to free you up from the little things so that prospecting never suffers. No matter what business you're in, as soon as you stop prospecting, your business is going to drop off. That's a fact. I've seen it happen to salespeople time and time again.

Additionally, if you work forty-eight weeks per year, wouldn't it make sense to earn $6,400 every week, for a total of $307,200 ($6,400 x 48 = $307,200)? Of course, some weeks would be better than others. But what if you averaged your numbers? You would be one happy salesperson!

So here is my challenge to you: I challenge you to go to your calendar and schedule twenty minutes tomorrow to figure out exactly how much each dial is worth to you. Then, figure out what changes you need to make to increase the worth of each dial. You can use the example I provided as a template to help you with the exercise.

When I was in fundraising, every dial was worth approximately $64. I even wrote a big "$64" at the top of each of my scripts. I wanted to keep my motivation clearly where I could always see it.

Finally, as you prospect, remember to reward yourself, not just when you close a deal, but also when you stick to your planned number of dials each day. Pat yourself on the back and generate a reward system where you accumulate points to take yourself on a vacation or buy something for yourself that would be considered a treat. A good friend of mine in Sacramento, Mike Brill, used to photocopy Monopoly™ money. Each day he would pay himself based on how much prospecting he got accomplished. Then, when he reached a certain amount of Monopoly money, he would do something nice with his family, such as a special dinner out or movie night. As a result, his entire family was interested in his success and would cheer him on to always do better.

If for some reason you just did not want to prospect and were convinced you could get a telemarketing company to do at least fifty percent of your production, wouldn't you hire them? Assume it took the telemarketing company thirty hours to set those ten appointments, and they billed you at $30 an hour, would it be worth $900 to make $6,400? I certainly think so. Once again, these are my numbers. What are yours?

Since we know that prospecting is the most important thing we can do in the sales process, schedule your prospecting time each week, and get it done before moving onto anything else, if at all possible. Finally, develop the attitude that if you ever reach a point in the day when you feel you have nothing to do, prospect!

Now that you know why prospecting is so worthwhile, let's cover some specific prospecting techniques. That's what the next three chapters will show you.

Notes

Chapter Six

Telephone Prospecting

One of the most common ways to prospect is via phone. And with the proliferation of cell phones, you no longer have to be tied to your desk to prospect. You can prospect while you're sitting in traffic, while driving to or from an appointment, or even from a sunny park bench on a beautiful Spring day. So there's really no reason not to prospect via phone.

Realize that when you prospect via phone, you need to employ key skills that will enable you to get in and actually talk with your prospect. Simply approaching phone prospecting the same way you would approach making a call to your mom won't give you the results you want. Rather, you need to follow some proven phone prospecting techniques.

Maintain a Positive Attitude

Having a positive attitude is critical. People can tell over the telephone if you are confident, stressed, pushing, etc. Therefore, don't get on the phone right after you and your spouse have a spat, or after you just heard that your stock portfolio tanked. I recall one time when I disobeyed this rule and had a rude awakening. A few years ago I invested in a thoroughbred race horse. Within a few days, I received a phone call that the horse got injured and would have to be retired. Not only was this unfortunate, because he was a great horse, but it was also a big financial loss for me. The horse had only participated in three races since I owned him, so I wasn't even close to earning my investment back.

83

Immediately after getting the call, I was in the mindset of: "Now I have to earn all that money back." Rather than give myself time to cool off, I got on the phone and started prospecting immediately. Partway through my first prospecting call, the gentleman I was talking to interrupted me and said, "Gary, are you alright?"

"Sure," I said, a little confused why a new prospect would ask me such a question. "Why do you ask?"

"Because this is Mark…Mark Johnson…and we've been doing business together for over ten years. Why are you prospecting me?"

Ooops! Fortunately, Mark was very understanding of my mistake. But that day I learned the importance of being positive, focused, and clear-headed before getting on the phone.

So before making any phone calls, pump yourself up. Listen to a motivational CD or read some inspirational story. Use the positive self-talk we covered earlier. Say things like, "I'm very successful on the phone and I'm good at this." Before each dial I used to say to myself, "Here's my next big client, yeah baby!"

I also recommend standing or at least sitting up straight in a good chair while you're on the phone. This allows you to be more, energetic, animated, and natural when you speak. If you do have to sit for some reason, sit forward in your seat; don't lean back in your chair. Sitting up will mimic standing so you can be more professional on the phone. Also, use a headset if at all possible so you can take notes more easily without straining your neck. Perhaps most important is to smile. I remember doing theater while growing up, and the director would always say "SMILE." Your whole body language and aura changes when you smile. If smiling is difficult for you, get a small mirror and put it at your desk. I guarantee you'll smile each time you see yourself. Besides, if you don't want to look at your mug, how can you expect anybody to listen to you?

If you have a few bad calls (rejections) in a row, call a client with whom you personally like to energize yourself. We all have those clients who are a joy to talk to. Call one of those people just to say "hello." The good energy you get from that person will get you out of the rejection funk. Or, if you can't think of a customer to call, call a co-worker and get advice from him or her about what has been working. Finally, when you have a gap of time between your calls, be sure to give yourself a meaningful break. Take a walk outside break, a soda/water break, a music break, an exercise break, a sports talk break, a chocolate break, or a chit chat with a friend break. Get away from the phone for a few minutes and rejuvenate. Just make sure you come back!

Be Prepared

Always have all of the relevant materials you will need within your reach. These can include your prospect list, scripts, answers to objections, calendar, Telephone Score Sheet (see chapter three), and product information for a quick reference if they happen to throw you a question.

I recommend using two binders to keep all your information accessible. In one binder keep your scripts, answers to objections, and product info sheets. In the other binder, keep your prospect list, hot list of who to call on, territory information, and various score sheets.

Follow the 3/3/3 Rule

When phone prospecting, observe the 3/3/3 rule. I learned this rule while at a Mike Ferry Real Estate Training Seminar, and it actually works.

The first 3 stands for 3 rings. When you're calling someone, and he or she doesn't answer the phone by the third ring, hang up. Why? At the fourth ring, you're annoying the person. One of two scenarios is likely taking place: 1) The person you're calling is on the other line and has to deal with your ring in the background (or your call waiting click), or 2) the person is not by the phone, possibly in the restroom, and as he hears your continuous ring, he comes running down the hall with his pants at his ankles.

The second 3 stands for 3 times. If you call someone three times and leave three voicemail messages yet get no response from the prospect, throw the lead away. The person is obviously not interested, and after three attempts, you are no longer persistent; rather, you're annoying.

The final 3 stands for 3 negative responses. If you talk with someone three times, and that person shows no apparent interest or has not set an appointment with you, throw the lead away. One word of caution here: If you are in an industry where you have few prospects to call on, then you may want to rethink this last rule. There have been times over the years that I called someone every year, because sometimes things do change. I remember one instance in which I made a call to a Home Economics teacher every year and made a joke of it by saying, "I am here for my annual 'no'." One year she surprised me and replied, "I am glad you called…" Then she went on to place an order for a $10,000 program, which was double of what a typical program was for me. Additionally, she stayed a client of mine for over ten years, giving me over $100,000 worth of business during that timeframe! That's proof that persistence can certainly pay off.

I should point out that if you are calling on someone who is very analytical, you may need to contact that person more than three times to get a decision. We'll go into more about personality styles later. But for now, realize that some people need about five to six contacts before they'll commit to your offer.

Develop a Gatekeeper Strategy

Learn how to work with gatekeepers (receptionists, secretaries, dictators!). When talking with a gatekeeper, make your answers brief. Remember, the gatekeeper is *not* the decision maker. Your goal is not to sell to the gatekeeper, just to get by him or her.

Keep in mind that every business person must communicate with the outside world. Refusal to do so would definitely result in failure. Therefore, the gatekeeper does not intend to eliminate *all* incoming calls. Your job is simply to make sure your calls are treated with importance. So when interacting with gatekeepers, create a sense of urgency. But rather than saying, "It's critical that Mr. Smith call me immediately," try saying something like this, "If you wouldn't mind telling Mr. Smith that he needs to call me today, I would really appreciate it."

Find out the gatekeepers' names on the first call, and when you call back, use their names. By using their names and being polite, you win them over. I quite often have a little gift for the gatekeeper, and if I am in the area, I'll drop it by for them. I will say something like this: "Hi, my name is Gary. I have called here recently looking for Mr. Smith, and you have been so pleasant and helpful on the phone. Usually secretaries aren't appreciated and I just wanted to let you know I appreciate you."

Realize that gatekeepers are trained to ask questions in order to screen callers. And whoever is asking the questions is in control of the call. If the gatekeeper has to ask questions, such as your name, your company, or what the call is in regard to, he or she is in control of the call. Therefore, make sure you identify yourself and state your phone number early in the conversation. As far as what it is pertaining to, if they ask, I say, "I have a couple of questions regarding (whatever it is that they do)."

Finally, if you are having a hard time getting any information from the gatekeeper, simply say, "Mary, I really need your help. My supervisor has asked that I get these information packets out to the correct people before Friday, and there is a lot of material that must get into the right person's hands. I understand you can't connect me, but can you recommend who I send the information to?" Once they give you the name you are looking for, file it away and try a different approach to reach your contact.

Be Strategic

The time of day you call is just as important as what you say. So if you are trying to get through to a VIP, try calling after 5:30 p.m., when the secretary has likely gone home. You may also try calling before 7:00 a.m. Quite often, successful people start early and work late. If you are trying to leave an important message and you know it will be on voicemail, call immediately after the office closes so your message will be the first one in queue that the person hears the next morning. People who receive lots of messages may not listen to all of them, or they may be interrupted after the first few of them. You want yours to be the first one they hear, because typically people write their messages down and act on the first one first. When you do leave a message, make it easy for them to call you back by saying your name and number at the beginning and end of the message.

Be Creative

Do you know what USP stands for? It means Unique Selling Proposition. What makes you different than the next salesperson? What makes you stand out? Whatever it is, that's your Unique Selling Proposition. And therein lies your creativity!

People love creativity. It shows them that you will go the extra mile to "get in," so you will most likely go the extra mile once they contract with you for business. Being creative requires you to really think—really think about what is going to get you out of the current situation you are in and into the situation you want to be in.

Set aside time each day for some creative thinking. When you are traveling alone in your car, turn off the radio and turn on your mind. Doing so will improve your creative capacity and will help you be innovative in your planning, scheduling, and business activities. If you have a tough sales problem that is causing you stress, try letting your subconscious mind solve it for you. Think about the situation, briefly before going to sleep. Often you will wake up in the morning with a solution. I like to call this "creative sleeping."

Some people actually have a dream about the problem they're trying to solve, and the solution they've been searching for is plain as day right there in their dream. Other people simply find that sleeping clears their mind, so that when they awake the next morning, their brain is clear and refreshed, and solving the problem becomes easier and creative solutions are much more accessible.

87

When I think of someone who was really creative, I think of a story I heard John Madden share with a few of us at a sales conference a few years back regarding one of his former players, Ted Hendricks of the Oakland Raiders. One day Madden went into the restroom and saw Hendricks standing in front of the urinal, looking into it with a puzzled look on his face. Somehow, he had dropped 55 cents into the urinal. He would look down at the money, and then look at Madden, and then look down, and then look back at Madden. Finally, he reached into his back pocket, pulled out his wallet, pulled out a $50 bill, and threw it into the urinal.

Madden said, "What the heck are you doing?"

Hendricks replied, "You didn't think I was going in there for 55 cents, did you?"

I guess Hendricks *really wanted* that 55 cents!

Another creative example is the fictional story about the toothbrush salesperson. As the story goes, a salesperson went out in his territory and set up a stand on a busy street corner and only sold one toothbrush all day for three days in a row. His boss told him to try something different and creative. So the next day the salesperson set up his stand and placed out some chips and dip. His sign read: "Free Chips and Dip." People quickly started to come over for the free snack. The first gentleman grabbed a chip and some dip and shoved it in his mouth. Then his face scowled.

He said to the salesperson, "This dip tastes like dog food."

The salesperson replied, "It is dog food. Do you want to buy a toothbrush?"

Needless to say, he sold quite a few toothbrushes that day.

While this toothbrush story likely never actually happened, it proves a point that being creative will earn you more sales.

Being creative warms things up. Sure, somewhere in this world are seven people who actually enjoy making dry cold calls. The rest of us would rather stand under a cold shower, fully dressed, ripping up $100 bills. By being creative you don't enter into such a hostile environment when you actually make the contact with your prospect. Your creativity puts the other person at ease, which makes the selling process so much easier.

Creative Phone Scripts

Be creative with the voicemail messages you leave for people. Here are several phone message examples that are creative and different. I have personally used each of the following examples. Some I made up myself; others I read about, tried, and tweaked. Some of these will not work for your personality, but some will. To make it easy, I have divided these up by those that are creative and subtle, and those that are creative but require a little more chutzpa to do well. Give a few of them a try! If you find some that don't work for you, try tweaking them to fit your personality.

Creative and Subtle

☐ "Hi, my name is _____ with ABC Company. I work with such companies as _____ (say the name of the prospect's competitors that you work with). My phone number is _____. I had a couple of really important..." CLICK. It is amazing how someone's curiosity is piqued. They'll call you back just to see what they missed.

☐ "Hi, my name is _____. I'm not with the IRS, I'm not selling insurance, I'm not looking for a job, and I don't want to borrow any money. But I do want to talk to Mr. Smith. Could you please let him know I called and that I have a couple of important questions for him?"

☐ If somebody doesn't return your phone calls try this: Do a little research and find out who the person reports to. When you reach the gatekeeper, say, "I understand Joe reports to Mr. Smith. What is the best number to reach Mr. Smith?" It subtly suggests that if Joe does not return the call, you will call the supervisor.

☐ If I have left several messages for someone who has a secretary, and that person has not returned my calls, I do the following. I call the secretary and ask for my contact. Before the secretary can say anything, I say in a low voice, "Is she still with the company?" It is weird how often the person calls back. When they ask why I asked if they were still with the company, I say, "Since I didn't hear back from you, I wasn't sure you were still with the company."

❐ If you have called several times and get no response, say something like this to the gatekeeper: "I know I have called several times, and there is a fine line between being persistent and being a pest. I hope I am not making a pest of myself." Usually they say that you are not making a pest of yourself. I then say, "Great, I wouldn't be calling so much if it wasn't important. Is there any way you can put me through? I would really appreciate it."

❐ Call the CEO's office and ask the secretary who you should speak with regarding whatever you are calling about. Then you call that person and say, "I was referred to you by the CEO's office." You are being honest; the CEO's office did refer you.

❐ When leaving an executive a message, say something like this: "I want to make you a hero, an even bigger hero than you already are. When you return my call I will tell you about the idea I have been thinking about."

❐ If you have a good relationship with the gatekeeper, try to find out the best time to speak with your prospect. If she says 3:00 p.m., for example, you ask to be put down for a phone appointment at 3:02 p.m. This will let the potential client know that you put a high value on every minute of his or her time.

❐ Another simple idea, but one that works, is simply using the word "need." This word increases the chances of people responding to your requests. Too often salespeople contact a company and say one of the following. "Is John available?" "Is John in?" or "Who do I speak with that ....?" These questions make it sound like you have never met or spoken with that person before. However, if you say instead, "I need to speak with John. Is he in?" You sound much more confident, and you sound like you and John already have a relationship.

❐ If you need to get information about who to talk to and have had problems with a tight lipped gatekeeper, call another department, like accounts receivable or the service department, and ask them for the information. If you act apologetic, like you meant to reach another department, they will usually give you the information you are looking for, as they are not trained to be a gatekeeper.

☐ Pick an enthusiastic sounding voice off of the voicemail directory and say something like this: "I know you are probably not the person I need to be talking to, but could you help me out.......?"

Creative with Chutzpa

☐ After leaving several messages with no response, say to the gatekeeper, "I need to know the correct spelling of Joe's last name. I am having a plaque engraved with his name for a special award." Usually the secretary asks what the award is for. That's when you say, "It's the award for the most unreturned phone call over the last few months."

☐ If you continually get someone's voicemail, and if you are willing to take a chance, try this: "Hi, my name is _____ _. You probably already recognize my voice by now. I assume the fact that you have not returned my call is a good sign. It tells me that you must be interested in what you are hearing from me, because you are probably the type of person who would have already called me and told me that you weren't interested. And because you haven't done that, I will be by your office on Thursday morning at 10:00. I will be making a special trip just to see you, so if you have no intentions on meeting with me, I would appreciate it if someone could call me before Thursday. If you need to reach me, my number is_____."

To be honest, I have pissed off a few people doing this, but more often than not they like my aggressive nature.

❐ When a gatekeeper asks, "Does he know what this is regarding?" You respond, "Not unless he is a mind reader. But he is going to want to know what I have to tell him. Can you put me through?"

❐ Finally, when all else fails, here is a fax you can send when the prospect is not returning your call:

Please place a checkmark next to the statement that best describes why you have not returned my call:

_____ I lost your message and forgot to call.

_____ I am just not interested.

_____ I think you're an idiot, and I wish you would just go away.

_____ Not returning your call is a power play, but if you beg enough I might call you back.

_____ I was waiting for you to call me back one more time, as I have been extremely busy. I am interested in why you are calling and look forward to talking to you.

The Call Back

If you leave a creative message, you have a higher chance of getting a call back. So, what do you do when that happens? How do you appear professional over the phone so you can actually set the appointment? Here are some guidelines to follow.

1. <u>**Say Something Meaningful**</u>: Your exact phrases will depend entirely on what you're selling. In general, though, you want to sound confident and polished. Do not compromise on this, because it only takes seven seconds to make a first impression, and you never get a second chance to make a good first impression. Furthermore, seventy-one percent of purchasing decisions are based upon the trust and confidence the prospect has towards the salesperson. Therefore, verbiage is so important. How smooth and professional do you sound? I always pose this question. "If you were calling you, would you buy from you?"

Here is a sample script you can use when a prospect calls you back. Notice the underlined words and phrases.

"Thanks for calling me back. I called you because as I understand it, you're the Director of Operations at XYZ Company. I work with ABC company, and we <u>specialize</u> in helping companies in your industry _____ (state what you specialize in). I am going to be <u>in your area a couple of times in the next few weeks</u> and would like to quickly <u>pop by</u> and show you <u>what other companies in the area are doing</u>. Is it typically better to see you in the <u>morning</u> or <u>afternoon</u>? Would <u>Tuesday or Thursday</u> be more convenient for you? What time would that be? Great. I look forward to seeing you next Thursday. By the way, I just wanted to let you know that <u>I am not a high pressure salesperson</u>. I just want to show you real quick what we do here at ABC, and <u>if you like it we can set something up to work together</u>. And if you don't, that is okay too. If you would like, <u>give me your e-mail address</u>, and I will send you over a link to our website and you can check us out before we meet."

Now, let's analyze the verbiage we just used.

❏ We say "<u>specialize</u>" because we are professionals in the area of concern. We don't dabble in everything. We are very good in the area that concerns them most.

❏ We say we will be "<u>in the area a couple of times in the next few weeks</u>" because we don't want them to feel too obligated too early on in the sales process when they haven't gotten a chance to meet, know, and like you. We want them to think: "If you are going to be in the area anyway, sure, come on by."

❏ We say "<u>pop by</u>" instead of "stop by" or "come by" because if you stop by or come by you may stay forever! But the word "pop" infers that you intend to be there shortly because you are going to pop in and pop out.

❏ We say "<u>what other companies in the area are doing</u>" because our human nature is to "Keep up with the Jones's." Finding out what the other guys are doing is a big advantage and a reason unto itself to set up an appointment with you.

❑ We say "morning or afternoon" and "Tuesday or Thursday" because we are only giving the prospect a choice of two positives. If you only give one choice and the person is busy during that time, you have not accomplished the agreement between the two of you. And if you are going to be in the prospect's area every day, you appear desperate for the appointment and certainly not successful.

❑ We say "I am not a high pressure salesperson" because it puts people at ease. It lets people know you are sensitive and aware of the fact that there are a lot of high pressure salespeople out there…and you are *not* one of them.

❑ We say "if you like it, we can set something up to work together" because you are letting them know you will be trying to close them if they seem favorable to what you offer. You are not just there to shoot the breeze and waste your time and theirs. You are there to conduct business and get something done.

❑ We say "if you don't, that is okay too" because we want to let them know they will still be our friends even if they don't sign up with us. People, by nature, don't want to hurt other people's feelings. A perfect example is how people do whatever they can not to reject you in person. They'll send an e-mail or leave a voicemail, but rarely will they tell you "no" face-to-face.

❑ We say "give me your e-mail address" because it gives us another opportunity to make a positive impression before our first meeting. You can now send a link to your company's web site and one more short message prior to your face-to-face meeting. Remember, every little thing you do gets you a little closer to your final goal—a SALE!

Now you might think that all this verbiage stuff is a waste of time. Well, realize that the elegance of your verbiage helps you smoothly get to your desired result. If you are all over the board with your verbiage, you subtly send the message that you don't know what you are talking about and you are not confident.

2. **Perfect Your Voice Inflection**: Tape record yourself. After you listen to how you sound on a call, ask yourself, "Would I buy from me?" I recommend that you purchase a wireless headset so you can walk around the room and express yourself freely. You want to sound as if you are having a natural conversation with the person, as if he or she were right there in the room with you. You want to sound like you are talking with someone and not into something. If you tend to sound nervous, try this technique: As you talk, stand tall and put all your weight on one foot and press that foot through the floor. It will quickly calm you down and make your voice sound richer and fuller.

3. **Memorize Your Scripts**: The faster you memorize and internalize your prospecting scripts the better off you will be. If you want to get better, you must practice your scripts and enlist the help of different role play partners. Depending on your skill level, you may only need to practice an hour a week, or you may need to block off an hour on your calendar each day for a month until you improve.

You can even put together a simple one page questionnaire to use as a guideline during the call. While you may know your material well enough, the questionnaire puts you at ease in case you get off track. I also like using the one page sheet to take notes on so I don't forget any vital information.

4. **Confirm the Meeting**: After you set the appointment, e-mail the prospect a confirmation. I suggest e-mail as opposed to regular mail because e-mail is easier to respond to. In the e-mail, let your prospect know what you hope to accomplish during the meeting. Also ask your prospect what he or she hopes to accomplish. Keep your questions simple. Don't make it so difficult that the prospect will not want to fill it out. Ask such things as:

❏ "Who are you currently using as a supplier?"

❏ "What do you like about your current vendor?"

❏ "What do you dislike about your current vendor?"

❏ "What is the decision making process in your corporation?"

Use the person's answers to help structure your presentation. If they don't send it back, still ask these questions during the presentation. Sending this message after the phone call helps makes you look more professional and thorough. It also gets you closer to the "yes" answer you want.

Dialing for Dollars

When it comes to prospecting, always remember your goals and your "why's." Why are you doing what you're doing? Why do you want certain things in life? Your answers to those questions will be the reason to keep prospecting.

Additionally, if you don't prospect, will you hit your goals? Probably not. Is it okay if you don't hit your goal? For most salespeople, the answer is "no."

Finally, think about this: How good does it feel to walk into a new week with a ton of appointments and no time to see anyone new, opposed to walking into a new week with nothing but an empty calendar to fill? Well, unless you enjoy the feeling of dread and an empty pit in your stomach, then you'll prospect every day so you can always keep your calendar filled and never have to face an empty week.

The bottom line is that the more prospecting you do, the more money you'll make, so make prospecting a part of your everyday routine. That's the only way you'll stay on top!

Notes

Chapter Seven

Prospecting
Via Mail

While telephone prospecting certainly is effective, it's only one way to prospect. You can also make a lot of inroads to "Gettin' In" by mailing or dropping off a creative marketing piece. But before you get excited thinking you can do a direct mail prospecting campaign rather than prospect on the phone, realize that many people view direct mail as junk mail. So even though *creative* marketing pieces can get you noticed, you can't rely on them exclusively. You will always need to do phone prospecting and face-to-face prospecting (which we'll discuss in the next chapter) to reach your sales goals.

Later in this chapter I'm going to give you some ideas for an effective mail piece. I have actually used many of these techniques myself, and I believe that my chances of getting the appointment really did go up as a result. But before we do that, I want to share with you two stories of how prospecting via mail can really pay off.

A few years ago I was sending out a marketing piece on a regular basis, and I kept track of my results. Here's what happened: I sent a "Gift Pot," similar to a gift basket, to Principals of elementary schools. My goal was to get in and talk with them about doing a school wide fundraiser. My gift pot was an eight-inch plastic pot filled with a few of our fundraising products. I wrapped clear plastic wrap around the whole package and tied a bow at the top to hold it all together. On the pot was a sticker that said, "Just planting the seeds for a great fundraising relationship with your school. Enjoy!" The sticker contained my name and contact information. Also attached to the top of the package was a pack of seeds for "Forget Me Nots" flowers.

I handed out forty of these gift pots. From that, I got an appointment with twenty-nine people, and I closed twenty-two of them. I had to spend approximately $20 for each gift pot, including the labor to put them all together, yet I was able to pay for all of the gift pots by getting just one extra deal. I invested $800 in this campaign and made $33,000—not too bad for an $800 investment. My normal numbers when I would just prospect by phone (which would cost nothing) would be if I left forty messages, I would get ten appointments and close five of them, for a total in my pocket of $7,500. I truly believe that the creativity made a difference.

Recently I received a creative marketing piece in my own personal mail. The piece came from Steve Kent, a successful real estate agent with Prudential California Realty in San Jose. Picture this: In the mail came a small white box, approximately the size of a can of soda. Inside were a handful of hay and a little folded piece of cardboard. On one side of the cardboard was the gentleman's contact information. On the other side was a note that read: "Finding a good Realtor is a lot like finding a needle in a haystack." He then attached a string and needle to the cardboard.

I was so impressed with this piece that I had to call Steve. When we spoke, Steve shared with me that this box is the first of six mailing pieces he sends out to expired listings. The total for all six pieces is $6. I asked him if he could tell me how long he had been doing this and what type of results he had achieved by doing so. He was very open with me and explained that he had been doing the campaign for approximately five months, sending out an average of forty per week, which meant he had eight hundred people on his campaign (for a total cost of $4,800). I then asked him if he would share with me the results. He revealed that as a result of the mailings, he had three deals already completed and three more in the works. Assuming only those six go through, he would make approximately $60,000 on a $4,800 investment.

Take a Risk

Sometimes if you want to make an impact, you have to take a risk. Following is one example of when the risk certainly paid off.

A marketing piece I have used several times is to drop off some warm muffins and butter from the local bakery for the decision maker. I ask the gatekeeper, "Could you please give these freshly baked muffins and my card to the decision maker?" Then I leave.

Prospecting Via Mail

A couple of days later, I return with more warm muffins and butter, and this time I also bring some jam. This time I tell the gatekeeper. "I know you guys are in a JAM when it comes to deciding on (your product or service). I want you to know that I have some really great solutions I would love to discuss with _____ (the decision maker). I have to run." Then I leave.

A couple of days later I go back with more muffins, butter, and jam. This time I ask the gatekeeper if I can personally deliver the muffins this time. Nine times out of ten, the gatekeeper says, "Sure." Just be sure to promise to leave a muffin for the gatekeeper.

Another technique I have used is a bit more expensive, but it pays off handsomely. I have two season tickets for the San Francisco Giants, and they happen to be real good seats right behind home plate. On three occasions over the years I have learned that my potential prospect was a Giants fan also. So I dropped off one ticket for an upcoming game. Along with the ticket I included a business card and note that said, "I would love to give you a quick glimpse of what I and my company are all about, as well as the second ticket to an upcoming game. There's no pressure, but if you are interested, please give me a call."

As a result, I ended up doing business with all three of them. They all took me up on the second ticket, and two of them actually said they would like to go to the game with me. Let me tell you, spending personal time driving to the game, as well as shooting the breeze and eating hot dogs and peanuts, really opened the door for a great business relationship together. It is almost as if we were friends before becoming working partners.

You could use this technique with theater tickets or concert tickets or tickets for any event that would be important to the person you are trying to build a relationship with.

Marketing Piece Essentials

Remember that prospecting via mail is just one approach. Don't fall into the trap of only prospecting via mail and ignoring the other prospecting methods—phone and face-to-face. Before you engage in a mail prospecting campaign, here are a few things to keep in mind.

1. If your prospect asks you to send something, ask, "Will you definitely read it?" And then when you send it, put a sticky note on it that says, "Here is the packet I promised I would send and that you promised you would read."

Many times people are just trying to get you off the phone when they ask you to send them something. Therefore, you want to find out what their true agenda is. To find out, you can say, "I would be happy to send you the information. Can you help me better understand what your specific needs might be first, so I don't send general information that misses the mark." Or you can say, "I would be happy to send you some information. If you wouldn't mind sharing with me, I'd like to know if you are in the 'shopping mode,' or are you serious about finding a solution to some of your issues? I ask this because many people ask for information without any serious intention to schedule a time to discuss their needs. Then we as salespeople, because we are supposed to follow up, try to chase you down, and it can be uncomfortable for everyone. Does that make sense?"

2. These two responses to their request for information will help you unravel the prospect's true agenda and will prompt a deeper discussion that will help you get in the door.

3. Make your mailing pieces bulky. Big and bulky mailing pieces stand out. As such, the decision maker will pick it up and actually open it.

4. Follow up, via phone, to all your mail prospecting. Do so no later than a day or two after you believe the prospect received the marketing piece.

5. Creativity pays off. Just like your phone prospecting, your mail prospecting must be creative. Here are some creative ideas:

   ❏ Deliver a box of instant oatmeal, instant coffee, instant pudding, instant mashed potatoes, instant glue, instant hair dye, and Minute Maid Orange Juice. Attach a note that says, "By using these products, possibly you will find an extra few minutes in your crazy schedule to give me a call."

   ❏ Send a tennis shoe with a note attached that says, "I just wanted to get my foot in the door." You can go low budget here by sending a simple keychain of a shoe or a baby shoe that you got at the flea market. Or you can be classy and send a full sized shoe in a plastic case.

☐ Send a basketball with a note attached that says, "I just want to bounce a few ideas off of you." You could also send a tennis ball.

☐ Here is a funny one that really does work. Send a crumpled up brochure with a sticky note that says, "Don't throw this away, AGAIN!"

☐ Send a box with a beach ball, sand, and seashells. Include a note that says, "Life is a beach, but growing your sales income doesn't have to be."

☐ Send a model airplane with a note that says, "If you are looking for a model game plan that will make your sales take off, give me a call."

☐ Send a bowling ball and an actual score sheet. On the score sheet write: "Do you want your business to roll right in? Then get a strike by working with me!" (Since the bowling ball is heavy, you'll want to hand deliver this one. Note: If you want some cheap bowling balls, go to your local bowling alley and ask for their "defective" bowling balls. You can usually buy them for about $4 each. Then use a cloth bowling ball pouch rather than a bowling ball bag.)

☐ Send a cubic zirconium ring in a small bracelet-sized jewelry box. Set the ring on top of a small piece of Astroturf instead of cotton. Include a note that says, "When you are looking for a diamond in the rough, our program (or product or service) is your answer."

☐ Send a pizza delivery box with all your important information inside and possibly a coupon for a free pizza. On the outside of the box put your name or company name and write something like: GARY DELIVERS. (Note: Call Paper Mart at 1-800-745-8800. They can make these boxes for you at a very reasonable price.)

❏ Send a marble and a rubber band in a little clear box with a note attached that says, "When you think you're losing your marbles about who to do business with, be flexible and give me a chance."

❏ Send a large envelope with a lottery ticket inside, as well as a compact disc that doesn't have a title on it. The actual song on it will be "Take a Chance On Me" by ABBA. And the note attached to it would say, "If you want to win big like the lottery, you have to take a chance on this awesome _____

_____." (Note: If you really want to win a person over, tie the CD to a helium filled balloon. Put the balloon in a box so that when the person opens the box, the balloon drifts up and the CD is hanging in front of the person's face.)

❏ This one works well, but it takes a bit longer to execute. You can use this technique to precondition the customer to accept the initial phone call. I saw an advertising company use this technique to drum up more business. First, determine how many people you want to target who are qualified prospects. The example I heard was a gentleman targeting one hundred prospects to sell his company's advertising services.

During the first week of the program, he sent each of the one hundred prospects a small box wrapped in plain white paper. The box had no return address. Inside the box was a sugar cube, with a small handwritten message that read: "Keep it sweet!"

During the second week he sent a similar package. Inside this one was a lemon. The note read: "Don't let it go sour!"

During the third week he sent another box. Inside this one was a piece of tin foil. The note read: "Make it sparkle!"

By the time week four arrived, his prospects were now looking forward to the package. This final one came in the same small white box. Inside this one was the salesperson's business card. The note read: "I will be calling you for an appointment."

Believe it or not, but out of those one hundred prospects, every single one of them set up an appointment with the salesperson. I don't know how many he was able to close, but I'm sure he was able to generate a lot of new business because of the creativity that went into the mailing.

The Direct Approach

If you are not the creative type but want to make your mailing program systematic and effective, you can use a simple four-step program, which is a "standard" in the sales profession. While the creative approach will usually get you better results, I realize that it's not for everyone. If that's you, then do the following:

Week One: Send a one-page letter to your prospects that describes the problems your product or service solves. Include a short testimonial letter limited to thirty-five words, and mention specific measurable results that the person has gotten from using your product or service.

Week Two: Send a brochure describing your product or service, and include your business card. A tri-fold panel type brochure works best and is easy to mail. If your company does not have a brochure, send a bullet point list of the benefits of working with your company. Be sure to use your company's letterhead.

Week Three: Send a one-page handout about your company, and tell your prospect what time you will be calling the following week to set an appointment. Use an odd time, such as 2:47 p.m., once again, to show that you value every minute of their time. If your company does not have a one-page handout, send a bullet point list of ten positive facts about your product or service—what makes your product or service better than your competitor's. Again, make sure you put this on your company's letterhead.

Week Four: Call your prospect as promised.

Do not do more mailings after those three. Wait at last a month before you do another cycle of mailings. If you can't reach the person when you call, leave a message asking if they mind you sending them more information in the future. Even if they don't buy from you now, at least you'll know you're not wasting your time or money by continually mailing them materials. Realize, too, that if you don't have a large pool of prospects to mail to, you'll have to keep up any direct mail campaign longer than if you have a large prospect pool to contact.

You can speed this process up a little bit by doing your mailings every three to four days apart rather than one week apart. Also, to do this effectively, you should have all your mail pieces ready to go at the beginning of the campaign.

Another simple mailing program to try is a "postcard campaign." I remember a few years ago I received a postcard every week for ten weeks from a local real estate agent. It was a very simple white and green postcard with his name, picture, and contact information on it. Each week he listed a different benefit of working with him. If I had been thinking of buying or selling a home at the time, I probably would have contacted him because his message was short and sweet, yet very professional. If he was that organized to get the postcard out weekly, he probably was organized in his business too.

Let Your Satisfied Customers Prospect for You

Earlier I mentioned sending a testimonial letter with a sales letter. Testimonial letters are great prospecting tools, as you can let your current clients tell your prospects how great you are. I learned "the art of the testimonial letter" from a good friend of mine, Tim Fish, who works at Great American Opportunities. Tim is consistently in the top five percent of salespeople in the entire fundraising industry. How does he do it? Tim works smart by getting his clients on board as part of his sales force.

Using Tim's philosophy, you want a collection of letters from what he calls your "champion customers." These are people who will brag about how wonderful you and your company are, making you look like the best thing since sliced bread.

Try to get at least one letter per customary objection you are likely to receive regarding your product or service. For example, if you commonly get the objection that your product or service costs too much, you would have a letter that reads something like: "I have checked out and tried several of your competitors, yet what they give you for your money is nothing close to what your company provides for us. I would highly recommend you and your company to anyone who asks."

You may ask, "How do I get these letters?" You simply have to ask. Say something like this to your champion customers: "Joe, I am in the process of compiling a series of letters from my clients, and I know you are very happy with our company and the service I have been providing you. Would you mind typing out on your company's letterhead a paragraph or two about what you like about working with us and that you would be happy to recommend us to others? I know you are real busy. So if you like, you can simply tell me what you like about us and give me a couple of sheets of your letterhead. I'll type the letter for you and then bring it by for you to read and sign. I did something similar for John over at XYZ Company, and he found it extremely convenient."

This approach works well if the prospect likes you, because now he or she doesn't have to take a lot of time to create the letter, and you can make yourself and your company look awesome.

You can use these letters you gather two different ways:

1. First, if you are having a difficult time getting in the door to a certain prospect, you can send the person four or five different champion letters, as well as a short handwritten card that reads: I would love to meet with you for just a few short minutes to discuss how what we do at our company could be of benefit to your company." Use a yellow highlighter to point out the two or three key sentences in the champion letter, because you may only have a few seconds of the prospect's time.

2. Send four to five champion letters to prospects with whom you have an appointment for the following week or so. If you have good letters, you will be amazed at how this opens the door for you when you arrive for the demo. When I've used this approach, prospects have greeted me by telling me what they wanted to buy and what they wanted to do.

On the next four pages you will find a few examples of champion letters Tim uses on a regular basis:

To Whom It May Concern:

It has been a real privilege to become acquainted with Mr. Tim Fish over the last ten years. I first became acquainted with Tim when I was seeking a fundraiser for my building. Tim initially impressed me with his sincerity and interest in developing a program that was best for my school.

I have experienced Tim Fish to be very efficient and professional as our fundraising representative. He presents himself well and works well with our parents, students, and staff. He motivates students to do a great job and reinforces our belief that students should not go door to door, keeping their safety forefront.

I am also impressed with Tim's willingness to assist in this fundraiser. Tim is here at delivery to assist with the distribution of product. When product errors occur, he is quick to assist to make it right. Under Tim's leadership, our school has benefited from profit in excess of $12,000.

It is without reservation that I recommend Tim Fish as your next fundraising representative.

Sincerely,
John Hunter
Principal
Brummitt Elementary School

To Whom It May Concern:

This letter is about our recent working relationship with Tim Fish and Great American Opportunities, Inc. Prior to our becoming board members of the PTO, our school used to do several fundraisers throughout the school year. Tim approached us with his particular program and said he could make as much money in one fundraiser as we had made with all our other fundraisers combined in the previous year.

It seemed a little ambitious and a maybe a little too good to be true, however we know that our parents would much rather support one fundraiser and do well at it than do many fundraisers throughout the school year. We decided to give Tim a shot since he seemed very confident that he could get the job done for us. To make a long story short, our first year with Tim we made over $14,000 profit which not only covered our entire PTO budget, but also allowed us to keep our promise to our parents to do only one fundraiser through the school year.

There were several things we really like about the program. First of all, we have had minimal complaints about the products and their quality. Second of all, each student's order arrived individually packaged and sorted by classroom. On top of that, the company offered a very rewarding prize program. With all of these things factored in together, not only did we have a very profitable fundraiser, but it was as easy as fundraising can get.

If you are looking to minimize your work and do only one fundraiser for the school year we would recommend that you give Tim Fish and Great American Opportunities, Inc. a try. Why do many fundraisers when you can make all the money you need with just one? I know our community and parents have responded very positively to this and I think most will.

Sincerely,
Brenda Matijevich
PTO Fundraising Chairperson
Lake Street Elementary School

To Whom It May Concern:

This letter is to inform you of my fundraising experience with Tim Fish and Great American Opportunities, Inc. I am a very busy choral director at Morgan Township School. We are a very small school yet we have a very strong and dynamic music department.

I worked with Tim for the first time this fall with a cookie dough sale. In the past, we have done a different type of sale and made approximately $2000 to $2500 net profit. In our first year with Tim's cookie dough program, we made a profit of approximately $7700. As you can see, that is an extremely large increase from what we had done in the past. I attribute the success of the program to a couple of key reasons.

Number one, the cookie dough is of extremely high quality and is very reasonably priced for the quality and amount of cookie dough received. Number two, Tim is very good at motivating the kids and getting them excited about doing a fundraiser. His presentation to the students relates to their level very well and they get very excited about some of the special incentives offered as well.

I also wanted to say that Tim was always accessible anytime I had any questions. I had his cell phone number, email address, and his toll free number. I felt like I could call anytime with a question and I would get a response very quickly.

It has been an enjoyable experience and most importantly, an extremely prolific one. Due to the exceptionally tight state funding that is currently going on in Indiana, if you are a music teacher who needs a great fundraiser I would highly recommend Tim Fish and Great American Opportunities, Inc. It has worked very well for our music department.

Sincerely,
Tammy Snyder
Morgan Township Choir Director
Morgan Township Jr.-Sr. High School

To Whom It May Concern:

This letter is to inform you of my working relationship with Tim Fish and Great American Opportunities.

I am a choir director at a school with a very successful and large choral program. I look at fundraising as a necessary evil. We need to raise money for contest fees, performance outfits, and many, many other program needs.

I have been extremely happy in working with Tim Fish and Great American mainly for two reasons. Number one, we have raised a great deal of money which is very helpful to my program. Number two, and probably most importantly, it is very easy for me as a choir director. I have a program with approximately 200 students and simply don't have the time for anything extra. WHAT I LIKE BEST ABOUT WORKING WITH TIM AND GREAT AMERICAN IS THAT THEY REALLY DO MAKE IT AS EASY AS FUNDRAISING CAN BE. I would also like to mention that the product we sell has been great. The community loves the quality and for the value you really can't beat it.

If you are a busy choir teacher like myself but you need to raise money, I would highly recommend that you work with Tim Fish and Great American Opportunities. They will get you the results you need, but most importantly, they will do it with the least amount of work and hassle. So, if you are looking for the very best in fundraising, look no further than Tim Fish and Great American Opportunities.

Sincerely,

Denna Broge
Choir Director
Twin Lakes High School

Money is in the Mail

So why do we want to consider using all of these creative mailing pieces when we're prospecting? Because we have competition.

Competition is a good thing, whether you're competing with yourself or others. Competition is a necessary success principle that pushes us to our maximum peak performance. The key is to do all you can to win.

I once heard a great story that illustrates this point. Two men were hiking in the mountains when they came face to face with a Grizzly Bear. The two men were terrified and knew they had to get out of there right away. The two men began running as fast as they could down the mountain trail until one of the men suddenly stopped. The other man was behind him, so he stopped too.

"Why are you stopping?" he asked.

"To put on my running shoes," the other replied.

"But why? You can't outrun the bear."

"I know," he replied. "But all I really have to do is outrun you!"

So I say, outrun your competition. Add these mail prospecting techniques to your prospecting arsenal and very soon you'll be gettin' in more doors than ever before.

Notes

Chapter Eight

Prospecting Face-to-Face

The final prospecting method is the good, old-fashioned face-to-face sales call. Now, I don't recommend face-to-face prospecting as your sole means of prospecting, because you'll be calling on "cold" contacts and will be receiving lots of rejection. However, if you are in the area, and if time wise it makes sense to visit the prospect, then you may want to do it.

For example, I used to do some face-to-face prospecting when I drove a half-hour or more to an appointment. To me, it didn't make sense to go straight back to the office after my sales call. I always tried to have more than one thing lined up in the location I was going, but it didn't always work out that way. That's when face-to-face prospecting came into play.

Since I was in the area anyway, I would arrive at my prospects' offices to see if I can make headway with a prospect. Realize I don't recommend just going business to business hoping to land a sale. I recommend going to key businesses where you can "drop a name" (as in, "I was just over talking with Joe at ABC Company and thought I'd stop by"). The key is to use your time efficiently and to prospect businesses and people where you have a chance of making headway.

The wording I usually use during a face-to-face prospecting call goes something like this:

"I'm on a mission to meet all of the _____ (auto dealerships, company CEOs, etc) in the area in the next thirty days. I was right around the corner with Joe at ABC Company going over (or doing) _____ (insert what

115

you talk about or do), and I know you weren't expecting me, but I'll be back in the area later today and again tomorrow morning. Would it be okay if I popped by real quick and showed you what everyone else has been really excited about?"

This wording tends to put people at ease, and many of them will actually invite you back to talk with them.

First Impressions Count

When you're prospecting face-to-face, the impression you make to the receptionist or gatekeeper will either get you in or keep you out from seeing your potential prospect. Therefore, always remember the following:

Dress professionally. This means being well groomed, with your shoes shined and your suit nicely pressed. Make sure your clothes are clean and neat. I remember going into a school office one day for a potentially large account. After the secretary announced that I was there, she told me that I had a big mustard stain on my tie. I was completely embarrassed, and things didn't turn out like I would have hoped. First impressions played a big part. And in my case, that day they didn't play a good part.

People make amazing assumptions about your professional credibility and potential performance based upon your appearance, especially during the first meeting. And regardless of your knowledge or expertise, if you make a negative first impression, you will have an extremely difficult time turning your image into a positive one.

While some of the following guidelines on how to "look the part" may seem elementary, I'm always amazed how many salespeople simply don't follow them. Therefore, here are the basics of dressing professionally to make a good first impression.

Let's start with the ladies...

1. Wear a skirted suit that's knee length, a pant suit, or a conservatively tailored suit.

2. Wear neutral colors that don't distract. Avoid loud colors like bright yellow or pink.

3. Avoid transparent blouses and blouses with low necklines or revealing waistlines. Keep your arms covered to at least the bicep— even better is to the wrist.

4. Always wear non-patterned pantyhose that are neutral in color and that coordinates well with your skirt or pants. Carry an extra pair in case of runs.

5. If you wear perfume, keep it light.

6. Use natural-looking make up and a pastel or clear nail polish.

7. Do not carry a purse if at all possible. Carry a briefcase for the necessary essentials.

8. Wear flat shoes or low to medium pumps in colors that avoid making your feet a focal point.

9. Wear no more than one ring per hand.

10. Earrings are okay as long as they are not distracting.

Now the men...

1. Wear a matching suit in navy, black, grey, or dark green. Either pinstripe or solid is okay.

2. Wear a white or light blue dress shirt that contrasts with the jacket and tie. Your arms should be covered to the wrist. Short sleeves or rolled up sleeves is less powerful and less formal.

3. Wear a silk or silk-like tie that coordinates with the suit and shirt. Subtle and simple patterns are better.

4. Your socks should be calf length or higher. Dark black and grey are the best colors. Choose natural fiber socks because they let your feet breathe easier and you don't have sweaty or smelly feet.

5. Wear conservative shoes that are clean and polished.

6. Wear a leather belt that matches your shoes.

7. Short hair is preferable, as is a clean shaven face. I had long hair when I started in my sales career—and I mean L-O-N-G hair. On my passport picture, it read: "Continued on the next page." That quickly changed when I saw success so closely reachable.

8. Minimize jewelry. Wear no more than one ring per hand. No necklaces, please.

9. You can wear a full length coat over the suit, but avoid casual coats.

10. Wear cologne in moderation. Spray it in air and walk underneath it. When in doubt, don't wear cologne. Carry underarm deodorant in your car if you sweat a lot.

11. Carrying a briefcase is fine, but the trend now is to carry a simple portfolio that portrays a professional image. You can have your name or initials on the portfolio.

A few final points to consider for both men and women...

1. Mimic the dress style of your prospect. If you are selling to a farmer or mechanic, you may want to dress a little more casually than if you are selling to a high-powered corporate CEO. You want to look like you know, understand, and can relate to your prospect. Dressing appropriately is the key.

2. Your hair, apparel, fragrance, and jewelry should not detract from your professional image.

3. Use a lint brush on your clothing before you go out. A lot of men and women walk around with a lot of lint and pet hair on their clothes.

4. Remove facial and body piercing if they can be seen, as well as cover up any visible tattoos.

5. Studies show that if you look tanner you actually feel more confident, resulting in selling better. Don't burn yourself in a tanning bed or out in your backyard; just aim for a nice glow. You can even use one of the many "tan-in-a-can" products that will make you glow with enthusiasm. Realize that being tan may not be for you. For example, if you're selling in Wisconsin in January, a tan may not be appropriate. However, if you're selling in Los Angeles, you may want a little glow to your skin. In the end, though, some of the most successful salespeople I know have a

very fair complexion, just as some are nicely tanned. So use your own best judgment here.

6. Make sure you don't have any spots on your tie or shirt/blouse and that your clothes are not wrinkled.

7. Your clothes should fit well and not be too tight or loose.

8. Make sure your breath smells good before meeting the client or prospect. Always have mints or gum available. Remember, you cannot smell your own breath, but others can.

9. If you like something your prospect is wearing, compliment him or her. Everyone loves a compliment. It is a great way to start a conversation.

10. Enter the building with confidence. You want to look excited and carry an aura of excitement with you. Even if you are not excited, if you act excited you will become excited. To develop a level of excitement, walk ten to twenty percent faster than normal, and SMILE. Smile so wide that you could eat a banana sideways. Remember, you have a right to be there. You are there to help them with your products and services. Look and act like the self-assured professional you are. I have managed several sales reps over the years and have often seen them come in fumbling with papers, not confident, and already losing before they ever started.

11. Stride purposefully towards the gatekeepers desk. Smile and make eye contact as you do. A spring in your step and steady eye contact communicates confidence, honesty, and sincerity, all of which are so vital to your professional image.

12. Have your business card handy, but don't give it to the receptionist unless he or she asks for it. I have found over the years that it is too "salesy" to walk in with your card in hand. Therefore, keep your cards either in your pocket or right beneath your presentation folder.

13. Once you have reached the desk, pause for a few seconds. Smile and say "good morning" or "good afternoon." The brief pause lets

you catch your breath and collect your thoughts while conveying an impression of calm control.

14. Introduce yourself and speak slowly and clearly. Say something like this: "Hi, my name is _____. I was wondering if you could help me out." I have found that a polite appeal for help encourages the gatekeeper to lower his or her defenses. These nine little words give the gatekeeper a feeling of importance and control. They also help develop a sense of camaraderie between the two of you. Then continue with, "Could you tell me who is in charge of _____?" Remember, arrogance and pushiness won't increase your chances of getting in front of your prospect.

15. If you are given a name, ask if that person is presently available. Because you are visiting without an appointment, be grateful for even five or ten minutes with the prospect. One of the biggest reasons for conducting cold calls is simply to get your foot in the door, so be satisfied if you accomplish that.

16. If the prospect is unavailable, find out when would be a better time. If it isn't too long, you may want to wait. If isn't for a couple of hours, you may want to leave to do more prospecting and then return to the person's office. I usually say something like this: "If you were me and you really needed to get in touch with this person for just a minute, what time would you come back or call back?" This works really well.

17. Ask if the secretary or gatekeeper schedules that person's appointments. Quite often the gatekeeper can and will. But you never know unless you ask.

18. Always keep a small gift in your briefcase, such as a candy bar. If the gatekeeper is helpful, make sure to get his or her name, and say "thank you." I usually say something like this: "I'm sorry; I didn't get your name. You have been so helpful, and I really appreciate it. So often secretaries are rushed and don't give people the time of day. By the way, here's a little something to sweeten your day. I just wanted to show you my appreciation." Then give the person the gift.

Get Out and Prospect!

One of the best benefits of face-to-face prospecting is your ability to actually reach people and form that human connection. When you're prospecting via phone, you can only reach a certain number of people, because you're playing phone tag and your calls are being screened. And although you can make lots of attempts, you cannot control how many people you actually reach. The same applies for prospecting with marketing pieces. You can mail a lot of them off (or deliver them yourself), but you have no control over how many actually reach the intended recipient.

However, when you're prospecting face-to-face, depending on the industry, you have a lot more control over how many contacts you make. Obviously, if you're tying to visit the CEO of a large company, you have to get by the gatekeeper; but if you're calling on a small business, you can walk in and see a manager or even the owner, because he or she is likely working in the store or office. So even though you're doing "cold" prospecting and setting yourself up for a good amount of rejection, when you do make that contact face-to-face, you're forming a bond that can last a lifetime.

Ultimately, it's the combination of using the phone, marketing pieces, and face-to-face contacts that gets results. As you reach people via these different methods, they'll get used to hearing your name. You'll become familiar, and your prospects will actually take your call or see you when you stop by. When that happens, you're IN. Now all you have to do is get out with a signed contract or order. The next half of the book will show you how to do precisely that.

Notes

Section Two
Gettin' Out

Chapter Nine

Know Who You're Dealing With

Now that you have set the appointment and have your "foot in the door," you need to take the proper steps to give yourself the best chance of walking away with a sale or contract.

One of the most important keys to selling effectively is the ability to identify and interact with various behavioral styles. Why? Because to be a top producing salesperson (and to get out every sales door with a contract), you need to adapt your selling style to meet your customer's buying style. When you connect with your prospects on this deeper level, you will shorten your sales cycle. And when your prospects feel appreciated, valued, and respected (all because you adapted to their needs), they will be ready to adapt back to you.

Steve Reiner, President of The True North Group, has created a program called "Navigating Behavioral Styles" in which we learn about the four different behavioral styles: The Fighter, The Entertainer, The Detective, and The Counselor.

Before we go into these styles, take the following short quiz so you can identify your own style.

Navigating Behavioral Styles

Step 1: Navigate through the ten groups of words below. In each group, assign a 4 next to the word that describes you the most, a 3 next to the word that is similar to you, a 2 next to the word that is somewhat like you, and a 1 next to the word that describes you the least.

___Assertive	F		___ Steady	C
___Optimistic	E		___ Competitive	F
___Neighborly	C		___ Thorough	D
___Detailed	D		___ Social	E
___ Rational	D		___ Aggressive	F
___Helpful	C		___ Inspiring	E
___Engaging	E		___ Obliging	C
___Vocal	F		___ Cautious	D
___ Congenial	C		___ Modest	D
___Courageous	F		___ Influential	E
___Organized	D		___Blunt	F
___Extroverted	E		___ Friendly	C
___ Considerate	D		___Enthusiastic	E
___ Persistent	F		___ Team player	C
___ Interesting	E		___Prepared	D
___Supportive	C		___Resilient	F
___ Adventurous	F		___Energetic	F
___Entertaining	E		___Thoughtful	C
___Pleasant	C		___Animated	E
___Disciplined	D		___ Strategic	D

<u>*Step 2:*</u> Total the points for each letter and write them on the lines below.

___ F ___ E ___ D ___ C

You likely have one category with a higher score than all the others. That's your dominant behavioral style. Realize that we all have some elements of each style within us. However, one behavioral style will stand out and be dominant.

Now that you have added up your score, which style are you?

The following chart will give you a quick overview of each style.

If you scored mostly "F" answers, then you are a Fighter	If you scored mostly "E" answers, then you are an Entertainer
The Fighter Tendencies • Results/Goal oriented • Needs action • Motivated by challenges • Fears a loss of power • Under pressure displays a lack of concern for others	**The Entertainer Tendencies** • People oriented • Expressive & Optimistic • Motivated by social recognition • Fears social rejection • Under pressure becomes disorganized
If you scored mostly "D" answers, then you are a Detective	**If you scored mostly "C" answers, then you are a Counselor**
The Detective Tendencies • Task oriented • Perfectionist • Motivated by accuracy • Fears making mistakes • Under pressure becomes overly critical	**The Counselor Tendencies** • Team oriented • Active listener • Motivated to maintain consistency • Fears change • Under pressure becomes overly willing to give in to others

Naturally, when we are in a selling situation, few people are going to be exactly like us. As a result, conflicts are bound to occur. However, if you are aware of this fact, you can make an effort to adapt your selling style accordingly. Let me give you an example of where you could possibly have conflict.

Let's say an Entertainer is calling on a Detective. Looking at the chart, we know the Entertainer isn't the most organized person in the world, and the Detective is very organized and detail-oriented. If the Entertainer doesn't do everything possible to prove he or she is organized and detail-oriented too, the Detective will be confused and frustrated and will buy from someone who does display those traits.

You might be wondering how you can identify your prospect's behavioral style. Here are some clues to look for that will help you.

The Fighter

- ❑ Their general demeanor is pressed for time, impatient, fidgety, and energetic.

- ❑ Their business attitude is bottom line and cut to the chase.

- ❑ Their appearance is usually to dress conservatively.

- ❑ Their tone of voice is usually deep, assertive, and loud.

- ❑ Their body language is shoulders back, head up, and tapping foot.

- ❑ Their office environment has lots of awards and plaques, all attesting to achievement.

- ❑ The question they ask most often is "WHAT?"

The Entertainer

- ❑ Their general demeanor is welcoming, friendly, and easy to talk to.

- ❑ Their business attitude is that they prefer small talk up front to get to know you; meetings often start late as they are busy talking to others and lose track of time.

- ❑ Their appearance is to dress more daring and flashy.

- ❑ Their tone of voice is high, enthusiastic, and loud.

- ❑ Their body language is very animated, wearing their emotions on their sleeve.

- ❑ Their office environment has lots of family pictures, awards of recognition, and a messy desk.

- ❑ The question they ask most often is "WHO?"

The Detective

- ❏ Their general demeanor is reserved and distant.

- ❏ Their business attitude is that they prefer less small talk up front; they are interested in details, facts, methods, and functions.

- ❏ Their appearance is to dress more conservative, wearing perfectly matched and pressed pants and shirts.

- ❏ Their tone of voice is even keeled, reserved, and unemotional.

- ❏ Their body language is reserved, distant, and unemotional.

- ❏ Their office environment is neat and organized; everything has its place.

- ❏ The question they ask most often is "WHY?"

The Counselor

- ❏ Their general demeanor is easy going, steady, calm, and a good listener.

- ❏ Their business attitude is that they like to go slow and get a lot of information. They need sameness, predictability, and security.

- ❏ Their appearance is to wear conservative, safe colors.

- ❏ Their tone of voice is low and slow.

- ❏ Their body language is welcoming, with relaxed movements.

- ❏ Their office environment has lots of family pictures and awards focused around teamwork.

- ❏ The question they ask most often is "HOW?"

Adaptability Matters

Now that you know the styles and some clues on how to identify them, you can learn how to adapt to each style.

The Fighter

To adapt to a Fighter, you definitely need less rapport. Don't beat around the bush or make small talk with a Fighter. Instead, get right into the presentation and show how your product or service will impact his or her bottom line. Be clear and specific, and give the person choices. If you disagree, don't argue your point. Rather, simply ask "why?" Be careful of power struggles. Allow the Fighter to vent first, which will make him or her more open to your message. Ask for the person's help in reaching resolution.

To build rapport with a Fighter, ask about accomplishments, his or her job, home renovations, and sports. If you ask the right questions, he or she will take the time to talk to you, even though a Fighter does not like idle chit chat. Often, you will want to establish rapport *after* you have met the person's need. A good question to ask would be, "What did you get that plaque or award for?"

During the sales process, the Fighter enjoys tackling decisions and keeping things moving. The quicker he or she believes your solution will provide results, the quicker a Fighter will choose you. He or she bases decisions on perceived bottom line benefits and on other high profile people who have bought from you in the past.

To influence a Fighter, take the details off of his or her shoulders. Be confident and direct, and don't use a high-pressure approach. If a Fighter feels like you are trying to do a typical sales close, his or her ego won't allow it. Give the person options and the final say on next steps.

The Entertainer

To adapt to an Entertainer, you need to quickly establish rapport. Be enthusiastic and energetic, and sell the big picture with lots of sizzle. Don't bore an Entertainer with details early on. Ask for his or her opinion, and take the time to "dream" with the person. Keep things fun and use stories. Be sure to mention all other people you are working with.

To build rapport with an Entertainer, ask about his or her personal interests, family, and hobbies. The goal is to get the person to like you. This should be fairly easy, because the Entertainer is easy to talk to and get to know.

More than any other style, the Entertainer will often base decisions on how well he or she likes you. A good question to ask would be, "Are you originally from this area?"

During the sales process, the Entertainer will shy away from making decisions, because he or she is so concerned about what others will think. The Entertainer often seeks out other people's advice to make a decision. When he or she has to tell you "no," the Entertainer will procrastinate the decision.

To influence an Entertainer, include key decision makers in the presentation. Don't confuse an Entertainer with a lot of wordy detail. Use illustrations to help explain things. Keep up your enthusiasm and fun style. If necessary, have him or her help you set an appointment with the decision maker to speed up the sales process. Make sure the Entertainer is present during that meeting as well.

The Detective

To adapt to a Detective, you need to be prepared to give lots of details. A Detective needs to see charts, graphs, and figures to support your claims. He or she is interested in facts and logic, and is rarely motivated by emotion. Be specific and remain as objective as possible. Don't be overly emotional when talking with a Detective. And don't force a quick decision; allow the person time to think. Be very specific about expectations, and always follow up and follow through.

To build rapport with a Detective, ask about organizational type of issues. He or she is a logical, no-nonsense type of person who is not into building rapport. A good question to ask would be, "How do you manage to keep so well organized?"

During the sales process, the Detectives will take a very deliberate, sometimes painstaking process of weighing the pros and cons. Because a Detective wants to make the perfect decision, at times he or she has trouble making any decision at all. However, once you present factual evidence that what you are selling will achieve the results you claim, the Detective will quickly make the most rational decision.

To influence a Detective, present your material with more logic and less emotion. Show proof of all your claims. Ensure the Detective that he or she now has all the available facts. Be prepared to show more detail, if requested.

The Counselor

To adapt to a Counselor, you need to go slow. Tone down your enthusiasm, and speak in a casual, personal manner. Be interested in the person and what he or she is doing. Always ask for a Counselor's opinion. Don't be demanding or force quick decisions. Be supportive and take charge gradually with the person. Be sure to discuss how the team will benefit.

To build rapport with a Counselor, ask about his or her personal interests, such as family and hobbies. The primary objective with this type of behavioral style is to build the relationship. The Counselor wants to talk about security and removing risks. A good question to ask would be, "How do you stay so calm and in control of yourself?"

During the sales process, the Counselor will reject anything that involves change. For a Counselor, making a decision to do something new can be a painfully slow process. In his or her desire to please others, the Counselor often needs help making decisions. To help, give the Counselor validation that's well established and conservative. He or she is less motivated by end result benefits if there is risk involved.

To influence a Counselor, reassure him or her of the low risk involved. Ask if you can supply any other information. Don't pressure a Counselor to make a decision; instead, give the person time and ask what you can do to help.

Adapt and Win

Now that you know this information, you can't use your style as an excuse for your behavior. If you are a Fighter, you can't say, "I'm sorry that I came off as abrasive. That is just me." And you cannot use somebody else's style as justification for prejudice.

Take a moment to write the names of three of your current prospects.

1. _____

2. _____

3. _____

Next, try to predict each person's behavioral style, along with one sentence of your rationale.

1. _____

2. _____

3. _____

Ask yourself:

◆ What can I do to become better at adapting?

_____

_____

_____

◆ How can I learn to appreciate and respect different people's behavioral styles?

_____

_____

_____

◆ What is my plan to get to know people better so that I can truly adapt to them?

_____

_____

_____

I challenge you to spend half an hour this week reviewing these questions and the four styles. When you do, you'll be able to easily identify the behavioral style of the person you're speaking with, and you'll adapt your selling style accordingly. In fact, if you do this in conjunction with memorizing your scripts, you will see your closing percentage skyrocket as you get out more sales doors with confirmed new business.

Notes

Chapter Ten

First Impressions Count

A rmed with the knowledge of the various behavioral styles (as well as knowing your own type), you're now ready to go on your appointment. But before you ever show up on your prospect's doorstep, you need to get fired up.

Remember, your prospect decided to talk with you because he or she hopes to "get something" from you. Therefore, you cannot bring in your baggage from your personal life, your office politics, or your last appointment. People want to do business with professionals who are excited about what they do, who they work with, and what they stand for. Whether you are meeting with an Entertainer, who likes expressive excitement, or a Detective, who likes subtle excitement, you need to first have some air of excitement about YOU.

So, how do you get excited and pumped up? Simple. Do whatever it takes to get yourself excited. I have seen and heard all sorts of things people do to get excited—things like jumping up and down, saying or yelling positive affirmations, high five-ing a sales partner, and playing music very loud.

Don't let any embarrassment keep you from getting pumped up. Remember that whatever you do to get excited, you don't have to do it in public. You can do it in your car, behind the building, and even in the restroom. I have a cassette party tape that I made up a few years ago with several fast moving positive songs recorded. I crank it up on the way to the appointment and usually sing along like a rock star.

When I sold books several years ago (and I know the students still do it today), we would go out to the coffee shop parking lot in the morning before our first call and sing *The Bookman song*. I don't recall all the words to the song today, but the lyrics went something like this: "It is a GREAT day to be a bookman. It is the best day I know. It is a GREAT day to be a bookman every where I go. Goodbye, no, never! Goodbye, doubt and fear. It is a GREAT day to be a bookman, and be of good cheer."

We would sing this song several times while dancing around, waving our arms, and hooting and hollering. We felt awesome after doing it and were ready to go for the day. We were excited and fired up! I would even recite the lyrics in my head several times during the day to keep the excitement going and stay pumped up.

Punctuality Matters

Now that you're excited, you're ready to make that all-important first impression.

When you show up for the appointment, make sure you are on time. I know this sounds elementary, but you'd be surprised how many salespeople are not punctual. Being on time is so critical because being late means you value some other event more than the event you are going to.

I live by the motto: "If I want to be on time, be five to ten minutes early. If I'm there on time I am late. And if I am five minutes or more late, then I am forgotten."

If, for some reason, you are definitely going to be late (perhaps you got stuck in unforeseen traffic, for example), make sure to call your prospect and inform him or her of your situation. And call sooner rather than later to show that you are courteous and respectful of others' time.

Whatever the reason for your tardiness, tell your prospect the truth. If you spilled coffee all over yourself on the drive there and have to run home to change your clothes, then say so. Don't make up an excuse (a.k.a.: a lie) just to save face. Your prospect will see right through it. Additionally, when you tell the truth you never have to remember what you said.

Most times, however, salespeople run late because they got held up at their last appointment. If this happens to you, simply tell your prospect: "I apologize. I tend to give a little bit too much service rather than not enough. And the client I was just with required a little bit more of my time. I'm really sorry. I'll make it up to you." This approach is effective because few people will complain about good service. So if your prospect knows that you spent extra time helping someone else, then he or she knows that you're bound to do that for him or her, should the need arise.

If you're running very late and your prospect can't see you at a later time and can't reschedule, then try the following:

- Offer to give a condensed version of the sales presentation as soon as you arrive. So if your appointment was scheduled from 1:00 to 2:00, and you arrive at 1:45, offer to give a fifteen minute overview presentation only. Then you can meet again at a later date to give more information and answer questions.

- See if the prospect can give you ten minutes on the phone right then so you can give a phone commercial of what you do. You can then mail the person the packet you were going to give him or her.

Granted, being on time is always the preferred scenario, but sometimes things happen. Therefore, always have a backup plan in case an unforeseen event causes you to be late.

Confidence Sells

When you walk into the office, you want to make a great first impression with your "future client." Notice that I didn't say "prospect"; I said "future client." At this point in the process, there is absolutely no room for negative thinking. This person will be a client!

Realize that your body language (which is a mixture of movement, posture, and tone of voice) accounts for more than seventy percent of your communication (some surveys rate it as high as ninety-three percent), although it is non-verbal. Therefore, you need to pay attention to it. As Ralph Waldo Emerson said: "Who you are speaks so loudly that I can't even hear what you are saying."

Let's briefly review each of these non-verbal cues.

> **Movement:** When you first see your future client, move directly towards him or her at a fairly quick speed, and maintain eye contact. By doing this you portray confidence. I have seen several people over the years see their client before the client saw them, and they tip-toed towards the client with their head down and shoulders slumped. What a lack of confidence that

shows! Research tells us that you only have seven seconds to make a good first impression. So be confident from moment one!

Posture: Stand tall with your back and head straight. Avoid tilting your head to one side or another. Your feet should be hip width, and your weight should be evenly distributed on both feet. Stand in front of a full-length mirror and take note of your natural posture. Then force yourself to stand with correct posture. Notice how the various parts of your body feel. That's how your body needs to feel whenever you're meeting with prospects.

Tone of Voice: Aim to make your voice friendly and positive. Doing so will help your future client relax. If you get excited easily and tend to raise your tone, be sure to practice your vocal skills so you can overcome this trait. Tape record yourself so you can hear what you sound like. If you find that your vocal skills need help, find a co-worker or mentor to work with you.

I use an acronym that I heard several years ago to remind me to portray a positive and confident image. My goal has been, and always will be, to get people to like and trust me. And the best way to do this is to SOFTEN my image. To do this I follow these guidelines:

<u>S</u> = Smile

<u>O</u> = Open posture

<u>F</u> = Forward lean

<u>T</u> = Talk in a tone that conveys friendliness, concern, and enthusiasm

<u>E</u> = Eye contact

<u>N</u> = Nod to affirm that you acknowledge what the other person is saying

Building on this premise, when you shake the other person's hand, use a wide, deep, and firm handshake, but not too firm where it hurts the other person. Make sure you grasp the other person's entire hand and not just his or her fingertips. Very often people make an impression of you based entirely on your handshake. If your handshake is too firm, too weak, or too dainty, you've already made a bad first impression and will have to work extra hard to get the sales meeting back on track.

<u>Important Note</u>: Only reach out to shake the other person's hand if you have a pre-planned appointment. If you are cold calling, offering your hand for a handshake is actually too threatening and makes you appear like a stereotypical pushy salesperson. After all, you're already intruding on this person's time (from his or her perspective). By reaching out for a handshake you're now intruding on the person's personal space.

After the handshake, offer your business card, even if you know the other person already has one of your cards. Why? Quite often, after the handshake, there will be a moment of awkwardness for your prospect, because he or she may have forgotten your name or company you work for. By handing the person your card, you put the other person at ease and avoid an uncomfortable situation.

Something I heard several years ago at a Tom Hopkins seminar, and that I do often to separate me from my competition, is to write "Thank You" on the front of my business card. I then say to the prospect: "You may have noticed that I hand wrote 'thank you' on the front of my card. I guess I am thanking you in advance for the opportunity to someday be able to have you as a client and fill your needs."

Impress Them with a Lasting Impression

As the old saying goes: "You never get a second chance to make a first impression." So make sure you take a moment before meeting your future client to prepare yourself. Really think through what you're going to say. Take a deep breath. Picture the first few minutes of the conversation. What are you going to say? How are you going to act?

Practice is the key. When I was in college selling books for the Southwestern Company, we would practice our approach hundreds of times with role play partners. We even had to practice how we would walk through the prospect's door—how we would make our first impression. This included how we knocked on the person's door, how we stood, how we looked—everything. That's how important first impressions are.

While you want every impression you make to be a positive and lasting one, don't despair if you fumble at first. You can still win the sale. You simply need to work extra hard on the other elements of the sales call. The rest of this book will show you how.

Notes

Chapter Eleven

Building Rapport

As soon as the meeting with your prospect starts, you must begin to build rapport. Numerous business and sales gurus have repeatedly said that prospects buy from salespeople whom they like, trust, and respect. To me, this means building good rapport. In my mind, no rapport equals no sale. When I looked up rapport in the dictionary, I found that the meaning was: relationship, especially one of mutual trust or emotional affinity.

The most important part about building rapport is sincerity. You do not want to appear phony in an attempt to connect with your prospect. You do not want to try so hard to get the prospect to open up that he or she feels like you are being manipulative or insincere. So if you make a comment about a picture on the wall, make sure your comment comes from the heart. If you ask the prospect a personal question, such as "how are the wife and kids," make sure you really care about the answer. Don't move on as if you don't care or are only asking questions because you feel you "have to." Engage your prospect; look him or her in the eyes; nod your head to show you're listening. Most important, put yourself in your prospect's shoes.

Always ask yourself: "What is the prospect thinking about me right now? Does he think I am really a caring and giving person who is concerned about his well being?" Often, what you perceive about yourself is what the prospect perceives about you too.

Rapport-Building Tips

Here are three tips for improving the first few moments together with your prospect.

1. Prepare your prospect for what will take place in the meeting. If the prospect knows what to expect in the meeting, then he will more freely open up with you and not be so guarded. If you can reveal early on a little about you, your company, your products, and possibly some third party people you have worked with, your prospect will tend to feel a little more comfortable.

    Remind your prospect how long the meeting will last, and then make sure you stick to that commitment. Even though you may have already mentioned this information when you set the appointment, state it again anyway. People are busy and often forget the details. Also give a brief synopsis of what you will cover during your time together, and ask if there is anything of importance he or she definitely wants to talk about.

    During this time, *always* ask, "By the way, I'm curious what I said or did that caused you to have me come out here and meet with you today?" It is amazing how often this one answer can be the key piece of information you need to close the sale.

    As you begin the rapport phase of the sales meeting, help your prospect feel what it would be like to own your product, before you even get into the "sales" phase of your presentation. Immediately offer pictures of your product and testimonial letters from others who are happy with you and your company.

    A great friend of mine who is an exceptional salesperson for *San Jose Magazine* is Collier Granberry. He explained to me that before he meets with prospects, he asks them to send him potential artwork that they might use in an ad. Since this costs nothing and they have not yet committed to a contract, people usually have no problem sending it in. Collier then quickly designs a mock up ad and brings it to the client meeting. Once his prospects see their potential ad placed in a mock up magazine, they almost always say yes.

2. Have a comfortable discussion before the meeting actually begins. Don't rush things. You have to build a little bit of a relationship before you begin selling.

Here's a great story about two brothers that illustrates this point. One brother was in his mid twenties and the other was nineteen. The older brother had quite a reputation with the ladies and the younger brother had a real difficult time getting a date.

After getting turned down one too many times, the younger brother asked his older brother for some advice. The older brother told him that he needed to build a relationship first by talking to women, getting to know them a little bit, and building the relationship from there. "It is not rocket science," he said. "First, if you hit it off at a bar or on the phone, ask her to coffee. If that works well, you can ask her out to a nice dinner. And if that goes nicely, you can take a drive up to the lake. I put a moon sticker on my dashboard, and when the woman asks about it, I tell her it's there because it reminds me of her—how when I see the moon I think about how beautiful she is with her flowing hair, romantic eyes, etc. That usually gets a big smile and sometimes even a hug from the woman. I then tell her how I'd like to be romantic with her up by the lake under the moon and stars. With that, one thing leads to another, and the game is on!"

So the younger brother decides to try it out. He meets a young lady, takes her to coffee, and then dinner. Then he asks her if she would like to go up to the lake. She agrees. Once they are there, he says to her: "See that sticker? That's the moon. Now let's get busy."

So as I said earlier, rushing things is not always the best thing!

All joking aside, before selling to anyone, look for common ground by asking questions. Finding common ground gives you something to talk about. Remember, people like to do business with those they like, trust, and respect. When you can talk about things that are of interest to your prospect, he or she will naturally tend to take a liking to you.

So what kinds of questions are appropriate? Well, you can ask questions about their business, their successes, their families, the weather, etc. I like to say something like this: "Before we get started, I would like to get to know you a little bit. If we are going to end up working together, it would be great to know a little bit about what you like to do and what motivates you. Of course we will get a chance to talk about your business philosophy as we proceed through the process."

One question that works especially well for me is: "Are you originally from this area, or did you move here from another area?" People naturally love talking about their hometown, so it's a great question to get people to open up and relax.

Another way to find common ground is to simply look around the person's office. Let's say, for example, that you see a picture of the prospect at a golf course with his buddies. If you golf, you can say, "I love golf. I wish I had more of a chance to play. I'm so busy in this job, any time left over I spend with the family. But when I do get out, I like to play the best courses. Which golf course is that one in the picture?" This simple question can spur a conversation in many different directions. The prospect might say that he doesn't get to golf much either, or he might say that his family is also very important. Or he might go into all the great golf courses he has played at.

If you don't golf, you can still use the subject of golf as a springboard for building rapport. You might say: "My father (or best friend, brother, cousin, etc.) also loves golf. You know, I need to get him a nice birthday gift. Where do you recommend I get him a gift certificate for a free round?" Or you can say, "I am thinking about taking up golf. Do you have any good recommendations of instructors in the area?"

Common ground can also be business related. You can take time before the meeting to do some research about the prospect and his or her company. Do this by looking on their website if they have one, or talking to other people you know in the company or industry. You can then ask questions about things you found of relevance from your research. By you showing some knowledge of the prospect's situation you show that you care about him or her (or even his or her company). People naturally are fond of being cared about.

Common ground is not only about the same interests; it is also about the same styles. You have likely heard of a technique called "Mirror – Match." People who employ this technique want to be on the same page as their prospect when it comes to visual and vocal mannerisms. For example, if the prospect smiles a lot, the salesperson smiles a lot too. If the prospect leans back in his or her chair, the salesperson leans back in her chair too. If the prospect talks fast, the salesperson talks fast too. I think you get the idea. Mirror (or match) whatever the prospect does so you have common mannerisms. The key here is not to make it too obvious that you're using this technique. You need to practice this so you appear natural and sincere.

By looking for common ground and mirror matching your prospect, you portray a distinct image about yourself—one that allows the prospect to relax and open up.

3. Create a no pressure environment. Within the first five minutes of the sales meeting, make your prospect feel at ease. Present yourself in a way that relaxes your prospect and is void of pressure.

In chapter six I revealed the no-pressure phone script that works when a prospect returns your call. Here is a variation of that script, which you can use to put people at ease when you first meet with them:

"Today I am going to show you what we do at XYZ Company. I am going to share ideas with you that I believe you and I will both feel will benefit you. If at the end you like what you hear, then we can set something up to work together. If you don't think what we discuss together today works for you, then that is okay too. It may not work for you now. But I want to keep the door open for a future working relationship together. Although most people who I show our program to end up doing business with us at some point, it is not for everybody. If you decide not to get involved, that is okay. I have several other people I am seeing this week. (If you can, show your calendar.) One extra client will not make or break our organization. The most important thing to me is that you are happy and that I am in some way helping you move closer to your desired goals. Does that make sense?"

I know this is lengthy. You can remove or add various sentences based on the type of person you are meeting with and the type of sale you are trying to make. No matter what you do to the paragraph, however, whether you keep it as is or modify it, your prospect must feel as if it is ok to say "no."

Build the Right Rapport with the Right People

Without some type of connection with your prospect, you'll find selling to that person very difficult. So really work hard at this part of the sales process. Any old salesperson can walk in and say, "Here's what we offer. How many do you want?" But you're a sales *professional*—and a top producing one at that! So showcase your professionalism by putting your prospect at ease and finding that common ground.

Now realize that some prospects may want to skip the whole rapport building step. And that's okay. If you sense you're dealing with a very strong Fighter, for example, who hates chit chat, then you may want to say, "Sounds to me, Joe, that you really want to get down to business. So let's jump in…" When you do that with the appropriate people, you're ahead of the game and, in a sense, you *are* building rapport with this person because you're proving that you understand his or her needs. And that's what rapport is really all about.

Notes

Chapter Twelve

Corral 'Em In Before Your Sales Presentation

Assuming you have built some great rapport, you're now ready to move onto the corral part of the sales process. Some people call this the pre-qualification question phase, but I like the term "corral," because you are basically corralling your prospect. You are getting them to the point where they tell you everything you need to know to best help them, much like a rancher would corral his horses and have them where he wants them. During this corral phase you are taking care of any objections they have before you get into the meat of the presentation—giving your sales presentation and actually showing the product or service.

During the corral you are on a fact finding mission, gathering insight into the prospect and uncovering your prospect's attitude and opinion about your product or service. Asking simple questions, such as "How do you feel about that?" or "Why is that important to you?" will get your prospect to reveal so much.

There are five different things to look at during the corral. The details of each may vary slightly depending on what industry you are in, but the general concepts are the same regardless of industry.

1. **What are the prospect's wants, goals, and needs?** If you know this, you have already won half the battle. Sometimes you have to go one step further than simply finding out what the prospect wants or needs by helping the prospect paint a picture of that want

or need. For example, when I was in the fundraising business, I always knew my clients needed money to fund a program. But I had to take it further. I recall one instance when I met with a band director who needed to do a fundraiser to purchase a new set of percussion instruments for his band. I helped paint the picture for him by asking a few questions like: "How would the band sound with those new percussion instruments at concerts and halftime shows? How could it help your recruiting? So, I guess you are saying that if you had those percussion instruments, it would definitely improve your program, is that correct?" Now he had an image in his mind of all the benefits having the percussion pieces would deliver.

The bottom line is that we must help our prospects visualize and describe their need back to us, thereby making the need more real for them. You may want to throw some third party names of what other people they know are doing too.

Take a moment and think about some of the questions you can ask to find out what your typical prospect wants and needs then.

_____

_____

_____

2. **What is the prospect's prior commitment?** Find out what product or service your prospect is currently using. What company is he or she working with? Has the company signed any contracts for the near future, or are they open to new ideas? This step is crucial, because it is very disheartening to get a prospect excited about your offering, only to find out later that he or she has already made a prior commitment to another company.

The process for finding out the prospect's plans for the future is very simple. Ask: "Do you have anything currently set up for fulfilling your needs? Will those plans fill your needs 100%, or will you need some additional help? If we had a product that could help you fill your needs at a lower cost and with less hassle, would you be remotely interested?" If you can get a "yes" to this last question, you are well on your way to getting a "yes" for the entire sale.

3. **What is the prospect's previous experience with your type of product or service?** If your prospect has never dealt with this type of product or service before, then you need to be more thorough when you explain it. If you know he or she is very experienced, then going into great detail would bore and annoy the prospect.

    If your prospect has worked with a similar program or product in the past, then you want to capitalize on what he or she liked and didn't like about it. If your prospect is very negative on a particular aspect, then show how your product or service can solve the problem and be better than what the prospect has used in the past. The main point in this step is to get any hidden feelings or problems out in the open. Only then can you deal with the issues. Your prospect's past experiences will uncover future objections. Just be careful to never insult your prospect's previous buying decisions.

4. **Who is the decision maker?** There is nothing worse than going all the way through your presentation and then hearing, "That's great. But I don't make the decisions about this. Joe does." If you would have known that information upfront, you would have had Joe in on the meeting or attempted to set up another meeting with Joe. Never depend on your prospect to relay your information for you. Why? Because nobody presents better than you do, and your prospect's job is not to sell your product or service for you—that's your job.

    Note that sometimes people will say they can make the decision and later pass the buck as a stall tactic to avoid making a decision. If they do this, you have not adequately sold them.

    To find out if you're dealing with the real decision maker, say the following: "I assume you are the person who makes the decision when it comes to _____. In other words, if I showed you something that you really liked, you would be the one to say 'Yes, let's go ahead and do this,' or 'No, I don't think this would work here.' Is this fair to assume?"

Right away you must establish the fact that the person to whom you are speaking has the authority to make the decision. By doing this you smoke out any objections he or she may give you later on when it is time to close the sale.

5. **Is the prospect ready to make a decision today?** You want to know that at the end of your sales presentation, if your prospect likes everything you have to offer, that he or she is able and ready to make the final decision and move forward. At the very least, you want to have made strides in the right direction and know the prospect is close to making a "yes" decision. The main point is to keep the prospect from procrastinating on the decision. By human nature people don't like to make decisions, because with a decision comes responsibility. But as a salesperson, you don't want people to "sleep on it," because they tend to sell themselves out of it overnight.

I always say to people upfront: "Tell me 'yes' or 'no,' but please don't tell me 'maybe'." Nine times out of ten, "maybe" means "no," and most clients don't want to hurt your feelings by saying "no" outright, so they say "maybe" to be nice. I would much rather have someone tell me the truth today, even if it's not what I want to hear.

Continue On or Move On?

I want to talk for a moment about the prospect who doesn't give you any positive feedback at all, from the time you set the appointment to the time you arrive for the meeting and even through the questioning process. I am sure you have had prospects who reluctantly set the appointment with you, and you knew you were in for an uphill battle before you even started.

I have traveled with many sales reps in various industries and sat through sales presentations for an hour, and sometimes even longer, biting my tongue because I could tell early on in the presentation that the prospect was not interested and not going to buy. Yet the salesperson kept selling away and doing all of the talking.

As a general rule of thumb, if the prospect is doing all of the talking, then he or she is probably going to buy. But if the salesperson is doing all of the talking, the prospect probably isn't going to buy.

Just like the California rule for criminals, I have a "three strikes and you're 'outta' here" rule. That is, I give the prospect three legitimate chances to engage and consider buying my product. If the prospect shows no interest, I move on. I will not spend more than fifteen minutes with any prospect if he or she doesn't pass the three strike criteria.

So what are the three strikes?

1. If they are reluctant about seeing me, then they already have one strike against them.

2. When I am in the rapport section of my sales presentation and I am sharing with them success stories of people they may know or who are in the same industry, and they seem totally disinterested, I mentally give them a strike two.

3. Finally, they get a third strike if their body language is closed and they do not engage at all when I ask them open ended questions. If all of their answers are short and they keep looking at their watch, then I know we are at a strike three situation.

Depending on your industry, you may identify different "strike" criteria. However, I find that these three items work well for most people.

Also, if the prospect only displays one or two strikes, but the behavior is extreme, you may want to end the presentation anyway and not waste anymore time. For example, if I'm in the rapport section of my sales presentation and the person seems extremely disinterested—checking e-mail as I talk, doing paperwork, walking in an out of the room—then I'll end the meeting right then even though it's only one strike. Use your best judgment.

When I feel that I am "striking out," I look the prospect in the eye and say, "Joe, I can tell that what I have said to you so far this afternoon seems to be of no interest to you. Is there anything that I have said that has offended you or isn't clear to you? Do you have your mind on something else right now? Is it that you are interested and we should reschedule for a different time? Or is the bottom line that you just are not interested and you would rather end our meeting and move onto something else? I really appreciate your honesty."

Being blunt like this forces the prospect to tell you where he or she currently stands on your offering and on you. You win two ways when you are direct like this. First, if the prospect asks you to leave, you can spend your time and energy in a much better place and you are allowing the prospect to do the same without getting upset at you for pushing him or her into something that's not of interest. Second, the verbiage I just mentioned commands an answer—an answer that will tell you what move to take next. If the person expresses an objection or concern, at least you will know about it and can carefully craft an answer that will move you closer to closing the sale.

Bottom Line: Don't stay longer than fifteen minutes if the prospect is not interested.

Ready, Set, Sell!

Now your prospect is good and ready for your sales talk, which is specifically geared to what you're selling. Whether your sales talk is something you have created or something your company has put together, there has usually been a lot of time, effort, trial, and error that went into it. So the sales talk is generally the best of the best. Regardless of your exact presentation, though, be sure you memorize your talk. Why? Here are three key reasons:

1. By memorizing a prepared sales presentation and knowing exactly what you will say at each moment, you can concentrate on what your customer is saying. If you give an impromptu presentation, you will find it difficult to cover every important point and ask timely questions. However, when you give a prepared presentation, you don't ramble and can easily stay focused. You save time for yourself and your prospect and you give a more effective and logical presentation.

2. Knowing exactly what you are going to say gives you a great deal of confidence, which is so important in selling.

3. Study after study shows that your sales will grow if you use memorized scripts. I remember one gentleman in particular who literally doubled his sales from one year to the next simply by following and memorizing his scripts. He gave the same number of presentations, but his closing percentage doubled.

How about you? Do you follow a memorized sales talk? Does your company provide a script to follow? Do you actually follow it? If you could grow your sales twenty-five percent just by memorizing your sales talk, would it be worth it?

I recently put my home up for sale, but then decided to stay put and remodel my home instead. A few months later my home came up as an expired listing, causing local real estate agents to prospect me. In one day I received approximately ten calls from agents, and I was amazed at the wide range of skill level that I heard from these people.

I realize that I'm probably more critical than the average homeowner these agents typically call. After all, I'm a professional salesperson, and I have real estate experience. For about one year I was very involved in real estate, helping my fiancé in whatever way I could, as she is an excellent Realtor. I participated in her Mike Ferry coaching calls whenever possible and gained a thorough understanding of the industry. During that time I also became very familiar with the real estate scripts and could tell when someone was using a memorized script or was just winging it.

Out of the ten people who called me that day, only four of them had their scripts and memorization down. And only two of the four had enthusiasm in their voice. The other six agents sounded awful. They stumbled over their words and didn't sound confident at all. I certainly would not have done business with them.

How do you sound over the phone? How do you sound when you are presenting? Have you tape recorded yourself? Has anyone watched you and evaluated you?

As you can see, you probably have lots of room for growth when it comes to your sales talk. If you find memorization difficult, here are some tips that can help.

1. Speak it as you learn it. If you read your script out loud, you will learn it more quickly.

2. Repeated listening to a tape recording helps. Just as you learn a song on the radio with repeated hearings, listening to a tape recording of your script over and over can help you commit it to memory. This tape can be a tape of yourself or of someone else.

3. Give each paragraph or key concept a one-word description to trigger your memory. For example, suppose the first paragraph of your presentation is about the history of the company. Your one-

word description would be "History." Then let's say the second paragraph is about your company's dedication to educating clients. Your one-word description would be "Education." Perhaps the third paragraph is about how you form lasting relationships. Your one-word description would be "Relationship." And so on through your sales talk. Then take the first letter of each "trigger word" and make a sentence or nonsense type word for yourself. With our example, we have H – E – R, so we already have our first word: HER. Perhaps with the first letter of the remaining trigger words, we can make up a sentence like "HER DRESS IS RED" or "HERRING TASTES GOOD" or "HERBINATOR." While this may seem silly, it will definitely help you remember the order and logical flow of what you want to say.

4. You can also take each of those trigger words you create and tie them to an object in a room in your home that you are most familiar with. By doing this, rather than creating a sentence or nonsense word to remember your presentation's order, as you did in point three, you create a mental image for each trigger word. For example, if the first trigger word you need to remember is "Born," and I was using my family room as my familiar room, I would take the first thing to the right when I come into the family room as my reference point, which is the stereo speaker. I then make up in my head an image that relates to those two things, such as: "A baby being born on the speaker." Yes, it's an outrageous image, but that's the point. Now it's memorable. If the next trigger word I need to remember is "Needs," and the object to the left of my stereo speaker in my family room is a dusty glass table, I think: "I need to clean the dusty table." So the first paragraph is about where the client was born, and the second paragraph is about his or her needs. You could continue this with each trigger word, using the familiar images from the reference room you choose.

5. Learn one paragraph at a time before moving on to the next paragraph.

6. Listen to Baroque or Classical music while studying. Research shows that we have quicker learning results while listening to music with a high sense of order (rhythmically and harmonically).

Bach and Vivaldi are two well known Baroque era composers. Tape record yourself speaking your scripts with such music on in the background.

Prepare for the Payoff

One of the keys to getting out with a sale is to always corral your prospects before leading into your sales talk. When you corral people, you learn their hot buttons and can steer them in the right direction. I've found that by simply asking some key questions before delivering the full sales presentation, salespeople can double their income.

Then once you have people hooked, and only then, should you go into your *memorized* sales presentation. So practice asking the corral type questions and definitely practice your sales talk. With these two elements under your belt, your success is just around the corner.

Notes

Chapter Thirteen

The Pre-Sell, Product Presentation, and Add-On

The next phase of the sales meeting is called the pre-sell. This is when you describe the product or service before actually showing it to your prospect. The pre-sell gets the prospect positive about the product or service, and gets the prospect ready to learn more about it.

To make the pre-sell easy, consider what your prospect just told you during the corral. If the prospect mentioned that he or she likes something in particular during the corral, then you need to focus heavily on that aspect during the pre-sell.

Here is an example. If you are a mortgage broker and the prospect told you during the corral that she needs a mortgage that will keep her monthly payments down to a minimum, because he and his wife are currently paying for two kids in college, you would spend a lot of time during the pre-sell explaining how your company has relationships with several lenders that specialize in low payment options. You would further explain that you have several clients who are in a similar situation as they are, and the benefit of working with you is that you understand their scenario and know what to do to best fit their family's needs. You can then pull out statistics and documentation about the companies you will be recommending, and reveal all the benefits of those particular programs.

Notice that you haven't yet actually revealed the product. However, you have pre-sold the prospect on your ability to deliver exactly what the prospect wants. You've given a solution to the prospect's problem or pain. Now that you have the wants and needs addressed, the actual product or service itself is secondary, yet the choice to go with you (because you have the magic solution) is obvious.

Realize that the pre-sell phase is not a long and drawn out process. In fact, your entire pre-sell should last only one or two minutes. Think of the pre-sell as the adjective to the product. The pre-sell makes your product or service "just a little bit better." For example, when you talk and describe things, you don't just say, "A car." You say, "A beautiful red car." You don't just say, "A day." You say, "A hot summer day." Your pre-sell helps your prospect see your product as more than just another "widget." With your pre-sell description, your product is now spectacular.

The points that typically require pre-selling include:

1. You (your credibility and your company)

2. Your product or service

3. Your price

4. Doing it now versus later

5. The prospect's need

The pre-sell for each of these items is similar to the mortgage broker example we used earlier. So regardless of what you need to pre-sell, the process is quite simple. The point is simply to get people excited before they see what you have to offer.

The Product Presentation

After the pre-sell, it's time to move into the actual product/program/service sales presentation. Realize that the presentation is really nothing more than preparation for the close. The goal during the presentation is to get the prospect to agree on several different occasions, so that when you ask for the final order, the prospect has no choice but to say "yes" and your asking is really just a mere formality.

The key here is to stay in control of the conversation. And you do this by asking questions that require a positive or "yes" response. You can use several techniques to get those "yes" replies. Here are the most common ones that work well:

1. **Tie-down Technique** – When you use this technique, you insert a question at the end of a sentence or statement that demands the person to give a "yes" response. The common questions are "Isn't it?" "Doesn't it?" "Wouldn't it?" "Aren't you?" and "Don't you agree?" For example, if you are a car salesperson, you might say something like this: "The fact that it is right before the summer makes it a great time to purchase a convertible, doesn't it?"

   You can also put the question words at the beginning of the sentence if you prefer, as in: "Doesn't it make sense to purchase a convertible right before the summer begins?"

2. **Question with a Question Technique** – When you use this technique, you answer the prospect's question with a question of your own. You do this so you can better understand where the prospect stands on an issue. When I sold fundraising products people would always ask me questions about the chocolate. I would get question like, "Do you sell dark chocolate?" And I would respond, "Do you think having dark chocolate as one of our products would help the sale?" If the prospect said, "Yes," then I would say, "Great. Helping you make more money with the right product mix is one of my goals." If they said, "No," then I would say, "Neither do I." Usually, though, people won't ask a question unless it's important to them for some reason.

3. **Double Choice Technique** – When you use this technique, you are posing a question with two possible answers. Either answer is a positive response towards moving to the final decision of a "yes." An example would be something like this: "It sounds like you are very interested in purchasing the convertible. Would you prefer delivery today, or would you rather wait until the weekend?" or "Would Wednesday or Thursday morning be a good time to pop by with your paperwork?"

4. **As If Technique** – When you use this technique, you involve the prospect as if he or she already owned your product or used your service. It lets you know where your prospect stands on the "idea" buying. For example, you may say: "Assuming you were to buy the convertible, where would be the first place you would take it?" or

"Would you keep the convertible in the garage or in the driveway with a cover?" By asking these questions you cause the prospect to visualize owning the convertible.

A phrase I often use is: "Let's just pretend…" For example, "Let's just pretend you were going to work with me. What would be some of the criteria that would have to take place?" This one phrase "Let's just pretend" has helped me so many times over the years make the sale because it forced the prospect to reveal his or her wants and needs. Armed with that knowledge, you have a fighting chance.

<u>Important Note:</u> *Never* overuse any of these techniques. If you do, your prospects will question your sincerity.

Sell the Sizzle, Not the Steak

Make sure during your presentation that you are always selling the benefits, not the features. Why? Because people make decisions to buy based on emotion, and then they back it up with logic. Therefore, when you're selling, be sure to target people's emotions first (by focusing on the benefits), and then justify the sale with logic (by touting all the great features).

For example, I mentioned earlier that I started in sales by selling reference books door to door. We had the best books on the market for helping kids study for their homework and tests. We actually called the big thick books "study guides."

These books contained all of the subjects the kids were currently taking in school. But the books did not reveal the who, the what, or the where. Rather, the books revealed the "how to" on the subjects.

The benefit of having these books was so that parents, who had forgotten much of what they had learned when they were in school, could easily refresh themselves without going back to school or going to the library late at night when the library is already closed.

On the other hand, the features of the book were that it had an extensive index, all the subjects the kids took in school, and questions and answer keys. But the parents and students did not buy the features of the book. Sure, the detailed index was nice, but the real reason they bought was the benefit these books offered—that parents could easily help their kids study, and students could get the additional information they needed to pass their classes.

So in this case, the emotion is the desire to excel in school. The logic is the practical way the study guide made school success possible. Always remember that people buy based on emotional decisions and defend it logically.

If you're not sure how to determine whether something you're saying is a product feature or benefit, try this: Whenever you're listing all the great things your product or service does, stop and ask yourself, "How does this (item you just listed) help the prospect?" Once you get the answer in your head, you can then say out loud to your prospect, "What that means to you is…" Even better, before you go on a sales appointment, make a list of all the great things your product or service offers your prospect. Then look at each item and determine whether it's a feature or benefit by deciding if what you listed gives the prospect any emotional value, such as better grades in school, more chances for a date on Saturday night, higher profits, the ability to look good to a boss, etc.

The Add-On

The final piece to cover before the actual close is what I call an add-on sale or tack-on sale. Every sales job I have ever done, from selling books to in home security systems to fundraising products, has always had a tack-on option.

For example, when I sold books, if customers bought the Volume Library, they also had the option of buying a cookbook (a gift for mom). When I sold home security systems, if customers bought the infrared alarm system, they also had the option of buying the wireless remote button, in case of an emergency. When a friend of mine sold a life insurance policy, if customers bought the policy, they also had the option of buying their homeowner and car insurance policies.

Just about every selling situation has an add-on option. Think about it…

◆ When you go to a burger joint, the clerk asks, "Do you want fries with that?"

◆ When I went to Ripley's Believe It or Not museum, I bought my ticket for $10 and had the option of also buying the program that goes along with the tour for an additional $3.

◆ And you buy a car or a piece of electronic equipment, you always have the option to buy the extended warranty.

In most industries these add-on sales always add ten to thirty percent to the final total. And if you do the add-on correctly, usually fifty percent or more of your clients will opt for at least one add-on.

Why are add-on sales so effective? After the buying impulse begins, your clients are very susceptible to purchase another product that you represent. After all, they already like you (as evidenced by them buying from you), so why not capitalize on the relationship?

I'm always amazed how many salespeople don't even try to add on to the sale, even though they have several products and services available that will further help the customer. When I ask these salespeople why they don't offer any add-ons, they say that they feel doing so would be "pushy." They feel as if the client has already purchased from them, and they don't want to come across as greedy. What a misperception!

If you ask for the add-on sale with the customer's best interest in mind and not the extra bonus or commission you will receive, you will be amazed at how many people take you up on your offerings.

So here are some questions for you to ponder:

- Do you have any add-on products you could offer?

- If so, what are they?

- Do you have add-ons but fail to offer them?

- If so, what's holding you back?

To become better at the add-on sale, write out a script of what you would say to the prospect during this phase. Try it out on some co-workers and ask for their feedback. Also, find out who in your company does a lot of add-on sales and ask him or her for advice. All the extra effort is worth it, because just a few add-on sales can substantially increase your income.

One Step Closer

You're getting closer to the "yes" you deserve. The next step is where your client decides whether to do business with you. If you've made a positive impression, set yourself up with good rapport, have done a good corral, and in an elegant way laid out all the reasons why the prospect should buy from you, then you're almost done with the sales process. All that's left is to close for the business. We'll cover that in the next chapter.

Notes

Chapter Fourteen

The
Close

The close is the most important part of the sale, because if you are not able to close, you don't make any money. When I traveled with all the different type of salespeople, each one closed a little differently. However, they all had one thing in common: They had to ask for the business in some sort of way. Some of the ways were low key and subtle, while others were direct and to the point. Some of the ways took months to do, while others took just a few seconds. Regardless of your industry or what you're selling, when it comes to closing the sale, there are a few basic principles you need to understand if you are to succeed.

When you first think about closing, you naturally think about the end of the presentation. In reality, professional salespeople think about closing way back at the appointment setting stage.

Earlier I gave you the verbiage to use when setting the appointment. To refresh your memory, here it is again:

"John, I am going to show you what we do at XYZ Company. If you like it, we can set something up to work together, and if you don't like it, that is okay too."

Then I follow up with this important question, "Does that work for you?"

When the prospect says "sure" or "sounds good," then I know that I have gotten my first minor agreement, and I am beginning to close the sale. If the prospect does not give me a positive response, then I don't even bother going on the appointment. It is a waste of time for both of us. I may follow up with the person a few months later, but right now he or she is not what I call a "ripe" prospect.

Once you are at the appointment, you will have several opportunities to close. You need to be armed and ready when those times come. At this point people often ask me: "When is the best time to close?" or "How can I tell when my prospect is ready to be closed?" Realize there is no "one size fits all" answer to these questions. Each situation is unique; therefore, you must be able to pick up on all the closing cues.

Closing in on the Close

Prospects say and do various things to tip you off that it's time to ask for the close. Here are examples of what prospects may say:

1.   Positive comments about the product or service. When I would flip through a brochure of fundraising products with my prospects, if they oooh'd and aaah'd, I knew they were liking what they saw. That's a signal of when to ask for the sale.

2.   Questions about the product or service. I was recently out car shopping with a friend. We went to a few dealerships and saw several vehicles, but I could tell he was not ready to buy because he wasn't asking any questions. But when we visited the Mercedes dealership, he asked the salesperson, "Do you have it in blue?" and "Do you have this same type of car in a convertible model?" As if on cue, the salesperson went for the close at that point, and my friend did indeed buy the car.

      Not all questions are equal in value though. Some questions a prospect has to ask, like how much something costs. But some questions really make no sense unless the person is interested. For example, a home buyer may ask the real estate agent logical questions like, "How big is the home?" or "What appliances stay?" But if the prospect is really interested, the questions will be more obscure, such as, "What are the neighbors like?" or "Where does the property line end?" These are the questions that should prompt a close.

The Close

3. Repeating information. If prospects repeat something you just said, they are probably interested. When helping my wife with her real estate business, we once had a client who twice said to us when we were trying to get his listing, "So, you think we can get $1,000,000 for the house?" My wife said, "sure" and moved right into the close.

   Realize that not all repetition is a closing signal. Sometimes a prospect may ask you to go over something again because he or she didn't clearly understand you. Be sure you know why the prospect is repeating what you say.

4. Speeding things up in the sales process. When you are working with a Fighter, you may hear something like this: "So, let's cut to the chase and get down to the bottom line." That's just how Fighters normally are. However, if you're working with someone who is taking it slow, and once you say something he or she suddenly wants to move fast, then you know you've struck a chord and need to move to the close.

Aside from verbal closing signals, prospects will also give you physical closing signals. Physical closing signals include:

◆ They look at the product again. Maybe they pick it up, feel it, smell it, or taste it.

◆ They intently read the paperwork or brochure that you gave them.

◆ They warm up to you and look more comfortable.

◆ They smile or laugh a lot.

◆ They lean closer to you.

◆ They take their glasses off and put the stem in their mouth.

These are positive buying signals because they show that the person has a definite interest in what you're selling. The more someone interacts with you or your product, the more of a connection they're building with you and what you're selling.

171

On the flip side, watch out for the following signs. They indicate that the prospect is probably not ripe for the closing.

◆ They lean back and look uninterested.

◆ They keep their arms tightly crossed.

◆ They tap their finger, shoe, or pen.

◆ They look at their watch or clock.

If prospects do any of these activities while I'm presenting, I simply say, "Joe, I hope you don't take this personally, but I don't see you jumping over the table with baited breath wanting to get involved in our program. Is there something I said or did that is bothering you?"

When you ask this question, very often the prospect will reveal his or her true concern or objection. You then know what you have to overcome to get the meeting back on track. Or, even better, the prospect will reply by saying something like, "I'm sorry. I didn't realize I was being so distant. I'm having a real bad day." Not that it's good that someone is having a bad day, but now you know for sure that it's not you who's turning the prospect off.

If you do not address your prospect's obvious disinterest, then you are wasting your time as well as your prospect's. If you get cues that the person is not going to buy, then don't keep presenting.

The Trial Close

The trial close is an important aspect to smoothly closing the sale. I define a trial close as a minor close to test if your prospect is ready to move further forward in the process. I like to compare it to what we all do when we go swimming. We very cautiously dip one toe into the water to see how cold it is before we take the plunge.

When you do a trial close, you ask questions like:

◆ "What do you think so far?"

◆ "Does what we have been discussing so far appeal to you?"

◆ "Is there anything so far that is of concern to you, or are we right on track?"

◆ "Are you comfortable with what I have shared with you so far?"

If the prospect's response is negative, then you have not caused a lot of discomfort to yourself or your prospect by attempting to go for the big close and getting shot down. So you really haven't lost any ground. If you do receive a negative response, though, then you need to get the prospect to elaborate on why he or she feels that way. Then you can get the person back on track with you and address any concerns before you do the real close.

> **A Word OF Caution:** Do not overuse the trial close technique. If you do, you'll appear very "canned." I may trial close two or three times per presentation, asking a different question each time.

Characteristics of a Great Closer

All great sales closers have a few things in common. They are:

1. **Great closers have a burning desire to close the sale**. They know that closing one additional sale per day, per week, or even per month will greatly increase their income. As I have traveled around the country with great closers, I have noticed that they often have a score sheet on the wall or in their car, and they can't wait to fill in the numbers after closing the sale.

2. **Great closers really believe that their prospect is going to buy**. Believing the customer will buy and selling with conviction greatly increases your chance of making the sale. Great closers expect success. They don't think it was just "their lucky day." In the car on the way to the presentation, they do a lot of positive self-talk, assuming the person is definitely going to buy. They say things like: "I am now pulling into the parking lot of my next big client!" "I know that I have the best product and the best price for this customer, at this time. Now I will prove it to be true!"

3. **Great closers are sincere**. People can tell when you are not sincere. Sincerity will always sell more than anything you do, and your lack

of sincerity will almost always kill the deal. Look people directly in their eyes and tell them how it really is. Listen and really care about what they are trying to accomplish.

4. <u>Great closers talk low and slow</u>. When you are calm and talk low and slow, your prospect will listen and believe you. If you talk too fast in a high pitched voice, you come across as pushy and tend to sound like someone they cannot trust.

5. <u>Great closers keep the close simple</u>. Your prospect must fully understand what you are talking about.

6. <u>Great closers ask a lot of questions that will elicit a positive response</u>. The more you get prospects saying "yes" during your presentation, the more likely they are to say "yes" during the close.

7. <u>Great closers realize the importance of names and examples</u>. They will "name drop" appropriately throughout the closing process. Once again, remember that the close is supposed to be a natural ending to your presentation that makes people feel comfortable to move forward. By using names of other people whom they know, you subtly make them feel comfortable because they feel they are not taking such a huge risk. After all, others they know have done well with your product or service, and so should they.

8. <u>Great closers never argue with their prospects</u>. They agree with objections and continue closing the sale. Whenever they must disagree with a prospect, they do it in a light, agreeable way. The rule of thumb that I like to follow is: "If I win the argument, I lose the sale!" One way to disagree in an agreeable way is to say, "I totally understand how you feel. I don't necessarily agree with you, but that is okay. Let's move on to the next point." If the disagreement occurs on a major point that could derail the sale, you could say, "If we were to work together, what would it take for us to move forward on this point?"

9. <u>Great closers never lose their cool</u>. They let customers upset them occasionally, but they never show it. They always keep their voice low and a friendly expression on their face. If you get the reputation

as a friendly sales rep, you can more easily build a large client base. Remember, more often than not, if people like you, they will overlook some of the bad points of your product or service.

10. <u>**Great closers are politely persistent**</u>. They are not overbearing, yet they give prospects a number of chances to buy before judging whether or not the sale will actually happen. The key here is to walk the fine line of trying a little harder to get the sale without the prospect feeling any pressure from you.

11. <u>**Great closers leave people happy**</u>. They make sure their prospects are in a good frame of mind before they leave. They want to brighten people's day. They are also aware that their reputation precedes them in the community. Additionally, they know that by leaving prospects happy, they, too, will be happier, thus increasing their chance of making a sale at the next appointment. When I walk out the door of a prospect or client, I always say to myself: "I hope he or she thinks I am a cool guy!" If the prospect thinks that, I will likely get to work with that person at some point in the future.

Some Real-Life Closes to Try

Now that you know all about the close, here are a few examples of actual closes.

"If I (we) can (summarize action to be taken), can you think of any reason why we shouldn't move forward with (summarize the desired act of commitment)?"

For example, "If we get you to save $1,000 every month on your mortgage payment, can you think of any reason why we shouldn't move forward with authorizing the paperwork so you can start enjoying the benefits of your new loan program?"

When you ask a question similar to the example above, you are not asking the prospect for reasons TO buy, but rather for reasons NOT TO buy. If you have done a good job explaining all the benefits of owning the product or service, then your prospect should obviously say, "No. I can't think of any reasons not to move forward." Since psychologically it is easier for people to say "no," you are subtly getting the prospect to say "yes" in a roundabout way

This process above isn't trickery. There are no gimmicks. And there is no high pressure salesmanship going on here. Best of all, this wording works regardless of your personality, or the prospect's personality. It works whether you are asking for the order or for another act of commitment during the presentation.

Here's another one for you. This one is great for when a prospect wants to "weigh things out."

"I understand how you feel Mr. Jones. A lot of people feel the same way you do. What has really worked well in the past to help people make a decision is to use what we call the Scale approach. We will write on the left side of the scale all of the reasons why it makes good sense to move forward with our program, and on the right side of the scale we will list the reasons you feel would be against moving forward with the program. When we are finished writing down the reasons, we will add them up, and the answer to your question about which way to proceed will be evident. Let's go ahead and give it a try!"

Give the prospect lots of help coming up with several reasons to decide YES to your product or service. I usually try to come up with at least five reasons, but I prefer seven to ten. Then, when it is time to come up with the reasons not to go ahead with your program, give the prospect no help at all. As long as you've given the reasons to buy in a casual sort of way, the prospect won't even realize that you're now being tight-lipped and not offering any reasons of why not to buy.

When the prospect is done writing, say, "Let's go ahead and add up our reasons. We have eight strong reasons to move ahead with the program, and only three reasons to not move forward. The answer seems pretty apparent to me. It always helps to weigh all the facts before making a decision, doesn't it?"

Finally, a close doesn't have to be a technique at all. It could be something as simple as saying: "Which purchase order will you be using for this transaction?" Or it might be something like: "Will you be using cash, credit card, or check?"

When we closed the sale at Great American Opportunities, we closed very casually, which I believe is the best way to do it. We would ask the prospect four to five questions in a row that all required a positive response. Then when we asked the final closing question, it was so natural for the prospect to move forward with a "yes" response. Here's an example:

Salesperson: "Do you like the idea of me coming out and talking to the kids?"

Prospect: "Yes."

Salesperson: "Is it appealing to you to have so many choices of things you can sell?"

Prospect: "Yes."

Salesperson: "Are you happy about the fact that we are a full service company and that we handle everything for you from the record keeping and pre-pack all the way to prizes?"

Prospect: "Yes."

Salesperson: "If I were to do the student presentations for you, would a Monday or a Friday work best for you?"

Prospect: "Monday."

Salesperson: "Well, it sounds like our program really makes sense for your situation. Do you have a calendar handy?"

Prospect: "Yes."

When they went to grab their calendar, I knew I had just closed them. In a way, this close is somewhat assumptive. But your potential clients like someone who is confident and willing to take a chance.

Right now, take a few moments to craft four or five questions that are applicable to your business that would elicit a very casual final closing sequence for your prospects.

_____

_____

_____

_____

_____

What's in a Word?

Be careful to avoid certain words that will bring your close from low pressure to high pressure. I avoid words such as "right now," "today," "tomorrow," "this morning," and "this afternoon," because they direct the prospect to take action right away, without time to think about it. Of course, we want them to take action right away, but we don't want them to feel pressured; we want it to come naturally.

Following are the most common negative impact words, and better alternatives you can say that won't hurt your presentation.

Never Say	Say Instead
Sign	O.K., Authorize, Approve
Cost or Price	Investment
Down Payment	Initial Investment
Monthly Payment	Monthly Investment
Contract	Agreement or Paperwork (Date Reservation Form)
Problem	Challenge
Pitch	Demonstration or Presentation
Deal	Transaction or Opportunity
Sell/Sold	Get them involved or participating
Objection	Area of concern
Commission	Fee for what we do or provide
Buy	Own
Cheaper	More economical or less expensive
Are you the decision maker?	Besides yourself, who else is involved in making the decision?
I think.../I don't know...	Let me check on that and get back to you. I want to make sure I am giving you the right answer.
I see your point, but...	I understand. Let's do this....

Close, Close, and Close Some More

Most sales professionals have two or three closes they use on a regular basis on all their prospects. For example, they may use one type of close if they're working with a Fighter type of person, and another if they're working with someone who is more analytical. Other salespeople have one tried and true closing method they use on everyone. The key is to learn what works for you and then duplicate that effort.

One final word about going for the close: don't be afraid to use more than one close on a person. If someone says "no" to your first close, retreat a little bit, address the area of concern, and then try another close. I usually do two or three closes before I accept the fact that the person is simply not going to buy no matter what I say.

Whatever you do in terms of closing, practice your approach and get *great* at it. The better you are at closing, the more money you'll make—guaranteed.

Notes

Chapter Fifteen

Overcoming Objections

Sometimes your prospect will have an area of concern (or what a lot of us call "an objection"). Objections occur because the prospect is fearful of something or doubting something you may be claiming. If your prospect has an area of concern, here are several strategies you can use that will make your client objections work for you rather than against you.

1. <u>Find some point of agreement with your prospect before you begin answering the objection</u>. You want to cushion your answer so that your prospect knows you understand the problem. Simple phrases like "I sympathize with you" or "I understand how you feel" work well here. These phrases let the prospect know that you are sympathetic, and he or she is not alone; others have felt the same way. Then answer the objection in a way that implies that once those other people heard what you had to say, they decided to change their mind and go ahead with the purchase.

2. <u>Look at the objection as a question</u>. For example, if the client says, "Your company's delivery time is too long," instead of trying to defend yourself and cause friction, silently rephrase the objection in your head to a question, such as, "Why does the delivery take this long?" Then you can respond to your prospect by saying, "Let me share with you the reasons why it takes that amount of time to deliver and why it is an advantage to have the services we provide."

3. <u>Turn the objection into a reason for buying</u>. For example, if the client says, "The advertising costs are more than we had planned on spending," you would say, "That is exactly why you should move forward. Our prices are an indication of the value our company would be providing you. With us you get superior quality and service that will more than double your results of what you would achieve with XYZ Company. Yet you are not paying double the price. Therefore, you are actually saving money in the long run." Now their concern of spending more than they had planned is definitely alleviated.

4. <u>Find out what the real objection is</u>. When they give you an objection, ask: "Besides (whatever the objection is) is there anything else that would prevent us from working together?" If they give you another objection, thank them for clarifying things and ask them again if there is anything else. Usually the prospect will give you the REAL objection last. Subconsciously, they don't want to give you the real objection, because they know you will probably be able to overcome it.

   Another way to get to the real objection is to reply to their objection by saying, "Oh?" Then if they keep listing objections, you say, "Is there anything else?" Again, the last thing they say will be the real objection.

   Once you know there are no more objections or concerns, you absolutely need to ask this next question. "If I can satisfactorily answer your concerns, would you be willing to go ahead with the program or purchase?" They are now committed to working with you if you address their concerns. So you better have your ducks in a row and have good answers to their concerns.

5. <u>Before you answer the objection, restate it your own words</u>. This allows you a little more time to think about an answer before you rush things and put your foot in your mouth. Wait several seconds before responding to the objection so you avoid creating an argumentative atmosphere. Additionally, pausing briefly and restating the objection lets your prospect know you are listening. Finally, it helps to avoid any misunderstandings between what their actual objection really was and what you thought it was.

6. Let your prospects answer their own objections, if possible. For example, if they say, "Your price is too high," you can simply ask, "Why do you feel the price is too high?" If they tippy-toe around the answer a bit, they might admit that their objection in not really that important. They may decide to not even worry about it any more.

To be a top producer, you should always be practicing and reviewing your handling of objections. If you really want to be a pro, you need to know every objection or area of concern that you are likely to get and have the answer on the tip of your tongue, ready to be spoken when it is appropriate. If you fumble through your answer, your credibility goes down the toilet and your chances of gettin' out with the sale decrease.

Some Real-Life Scenarios

Let's tackle a few common objections that we get across the board in several different industries, as well as the appropriate response to each.

Prospect: "I am happy with my current supplier."
Salesperson: "I certainly understand that. Probably ninety percent of the people I speak with are happy with their current suppliers. I have a couple of ideas here. Since it seems that you like what I have told you today, why don't you let me give you a quote for the next purchase you are going to make? If nothing else, it will confirm that you are getting the best available price out there. Does that sound fair? If I can beat the price, without compromising on the quality or value you are currently receiving, would you consider trying us out one time? If it doesn't work out, you can always go back to your last supplier.

Prospect: "I want to think it over."
Salesperson: "I can appreciate that. Joe and Mary said the same thing last evening. But after we talked about it, they felt a lot better and decided to move forward. I know that you wouldn't want to think it over unless you truly were interested, correct? I mean, you aren't just saying this so that tomorrow, when I call you to follow up, it will be easier to tell me 'no' over the phone than it is to tell me today in person, right? Let me ask you, what exactly do you need to think about? Is it the quality of the service that I would provide for you? Is it something I have forgotten to cover? Is it the cost of the product? (They

will almost always say "no" to the first two questions here and "yes" to the third, and you can usually overcome the price objection if you go back and build value.) If it is not the service, something I have forgotten to cover, or the cost, would you mind sharing it with me so I can think it over too? Possibly I can come up with a few solutions to your concerns if I truly know what they are."

Prospect: "It costs too much."
Salesperson: "I understand how you feel. A lot of people that I speak with have had that same concern over the years, yet they still ended up doing business with us because we were able to figure out a way to make it work to their liking. I was wondering, how much more expensive do you feel our product is? (Let them answer.) So if it was $___ (state a price that matches what they said) you would go ahead and purchase it, am I correct? Besides the price, is there anything else that is of concern to you and standing in the way of you moving forward? (They will say "no.") Great. Then let's see what we can do to work on the price." (Now go back and show value and need. Also, break the price down to the ridiculous and show it is only a few pennies more a day than what they are willing to pay or what the competitor is charging, yet they get all of these other options and benefits. For example, if it's $1,000 more for your product, and the shelf life is an average of three years, that's only about $1 a day.)

Prospect: "How much does it cost?" (In an objection type of tone.)
Salesperson: "Well, that depends on a few things." (Then be silent. After a few moments of silence, they will usually say, "Depends on what?" Then you continue.) "Well, it depends on (list several different options they can choose from)."

For example, when I was in the fundraising business, people would ask me what the profit percent was for our fundraising programs, which is similar to the "how much does it cost" question. I would say, "That depends on whether you are selling chocolate or cookie dough, and whether you want the company to handle all of the record keeping and packaging or you would rather do it yourself. Also, if you want us to handle the prizes to make things easier on you, we can do that too."

Basically you are telling the prospect that the bigger the package or more product they buy, the more it will cost. Never offer just one price for one product. Always offer more choices and you will be more successful.

You can also respond to the "how much does it cost" question with a question in return. For example, you could say, "How much do you think a *very useful* (or other positive adjective) product like this should sell for?" Make sure to stress the adjective you put in front of your product!

Solidify the Sale

Assuming that you have answered all of their objections and concerns, and have filled out all of the appropriate paperwork, you have a few more steps to take before you can officially get out with a sale. First, you need to solidify the sale. The worst thing that can happen, especially emotionally, is to think you just got a sale in the bag, and the next day or next month find out that the client cancelled for some reason.

So, before your client leaves your presence or gets off of the telephone, say something like this: "I am very excited to be working with you, Joe. I will begin to put all of the information you have provided me in the system. Additionally, I will order the appropriate materials, manpower, and anything else required to fulfill your order. And I am going to put you on my calendar to follow up with you on the following dates (list the dates). Before we finish up today, is there anything you can think of that might prevent us from making this transaction run like clockwork? If by small chance there is, I would love to address your concern today so that I can prepare appropriately."

By asking this question, you are at least aware of any loose ends that are still dangling. And if you know about them, you have a good chance of taking care of them. Too many salespeople are so excited they got the sale that they don't even want to ask the solidification question because they fear they may hear something they don't want to hear. But in reality, this solidification question will make you feel great because the sale is a lot more solid when they tell you, "No, everything should go through pretty well, and I look forward to working with you too."

Besides the solidification question, you definitely want to follow up with a letter or e-mail reconfirming what you will be doing and stating that you have started the ball rolling on whatever product or service you are providing for them. Let them know you are investing time and money into their account. This way, if they are on the fence for any reason they will let you know early before you have invested too many resources. I also enjoy including a few of my champion letters in with the follow up letter to remind them that they are making a good decision and will be happy, just as others have verified in the letters.

Finally, don't forget to call the client regularly during all parts of the transaction, unless he or she has specifically said such contact wasn't necessary. Follow up on promises and provide updates and/or status reports if something changes. I know sales reps who may follow up as many as four times in the first two months.

Overcome Objections to Solidify the Sale

As you can see, objections are nothing to fear; they are simply the prospect's way of telling you that you need to give more information. When you view objections in this light, you'll actually enjoy getting them, because then you'll have the information you need to move onto the solidification process.

The key is to know your objections like the back of your hand. When they say "A," you say "B." You should be able to recite your top objections and the answer to each in your sleep. Furthermore, solidifying the sale should be something you do every single time. Do not take any potential sale for granted, and do not be afraid if the prospect tells you about some hitches that may happen. After all, you can't address your new client's concerns unless you know about them. When you have this post-sales process down pat, you'll be able to enjoy more moments of glory from a job well done.

Notes

Chapter Sixteen

Getting Referrals

If you have done a good enough job to get the sale, then you should be able to get your new client to give you a referral. Some people may not feel comfortable enough to give a referral until they have actually seen you in action; however, if you ask correctly, you will see success.

You want to treat your clients so well that they would always feel comfortable referring you. I was impressed when I traveled with Gary Cruff of Ameriprise. At one point during the day I asked Gary, "Would every one of your clients be happy to give you a referral?"

"Let me show you something," he said. He pointed to his file cabinets, where he had eleven drawers of client folders. "Pick a number between one and eleven."

"Okay, six."

"Now pick a number between one and ten."

"Five," I said.

Gary then went to drawer six and pulled out file five. He looked up the client's phone number and dialed the lady. When she answered, he said, "Hi Lisa. This is Gary with Ameriprise. I have a potential client in my office here. I was wondering if you could tell him about your experiences working with me and with Ameriprise. I'm going to hand the phone to him and step out of the room so you are not uncomfortable."

I got on the phone with Lisa, and she went on to give Gary and Ameriprise a raving review.

Gary later explained to me that he treats his clients like family. He would want to be able to have a meal and feel comfortable with everybody he works with.

It's All in the Asking

In order to receive referrals, you have to ask. While some clients will always pass your name onto others, in most cases you'll need to ask for the referral to grow your business. Here are some tips on asking for and receiving referrals.

1. Let people know early in the presentation that a big part of your client base comes from and is dependant upon receiving referrals. Continue letting them know that at the end of the presentation, if they are comfortable enough to consider working with you, then you are going to ask them who else they know who might also need the services you provide.

2. Some salespeople let their clients know that getting referrals is part of their compensation plan, not something on top of it. They may tell clients, "In order to hit my company's goals, as well as my own personal goals, I need two to four referrals from everyone I meet." If people like you they will want to help you.

3. Many sales reps will offer some sort of bonus, gift, or discount for every referral they get or for every referral who ends up becoming a client. It could be a smaller item if it is just a referral and become a very nice perk if the referral actually ends up doing business with you. When I worked at Great American Opportunities, the fundraising company, I would give people a $25 shopping spree from our catalogs (which only cost me $7.50) for every qualified referral, and a $100 shopping spree from our catalogs (which only cost me about $30) for every referral they gave me who became an eventual client. The key is to only reward qualified referrals. These are referrals your client knows, and they wouldn't mind putting in a good word for you. You'd be amazed how well this works. I had one teacher who called me weekly with referrals. Her classroom looked like a gift store with all of the goodies she was able to acquire through my referral program.

4. Some salespeople call their new and existing clients several times after a sale. Each call has a purpose. The first may be to check on their satisfaction of product so far and answer any questions they may have. The second will be to share information about a new product that just came out. The third may be to ask for the names of friends, co-workers, or associates who may also be interested

in the product or service. Realize that the more clients hear from you, the more likely they are to help you find others to work with. This is especially the case if they are happy with you and your product or service so far.

5. Sometimes you will need to help your clients think of who would be a good referral. If you simply ask, "Who else do you know that might be interested in this product or service?" you may get an answer of "I don't know." Rather, if you ask questions like, "Who do you eat lunch with at work?" or "Who are you and your wife's three closest acquaintances?" then you are able to jog their memory so they can more easily think of a person to refer you to.

6. Another way to ask for referrals is to use the following wording: "Jan, if you were my mother and you knew that referrals were essential to my success, who could you think of that might benefit from what I offer?" This approach works well with people you are very comfortable with. And usually when you say, "If you were my mother," or "If you were my father," the other person laughs. When you can get someone to laugh, you put the person at ease, which makes getting referrals so much easier.

7. If you want to get referrals, it sometimes pays great dividends to give them. We have all heard the phrase "the more you give the more you get." This is so true in sales. One of my real estate clients was a great contractor. I referred several people to him who needed his services. He was very appreciative for the referrals. As a result, I never needed to ask him for referrals. He always voluntarily listed three or four people he knew who were looking to either buy or sell a home.

8. If you want to take a referral to the next level try this: Once a client gives you a name, ask if he or she would give that person a call to break the ice and tell how efficient you are at what you do and that he or she had recommended you. Ask your client to tell the referral that you will be getting in contact with him or her soon. This turns a cold call into a warm call and gives you a better chance of getting your foot in the door.

9. If someone says "no" to your product or service, but you can tell that the person still likes you, you may be able to get a referral. Say

to the person, "I am sorry that what we talked about today won't currently fit your needs. But were you at least somewhat impressed with the way I have handled myself and the presentation of the materials?" The prospect will usually say, "It wasn't you. You did great." If so, then say, "Since you seem to like me and what we are doing, I assume you would not mind referring others to me who may have needs that are similar to your needs, would you? Who might you know who needs…"

10. Finally, a great way to ask for referrals is by saying, "I have set a very high goal for myself this year, and pounding the pavement and working the phones alone will not help me get there. I must get several referrals from my friends and clients to help me hit my lofty goal. Everybody has been so helpful in putting some thought into who they know who could use this product or service. So I was wondering who do you know who…?" People naturally want to help others achieve their goals and dreams, especially if they like you!

Get Out with More than Just the Sale
Get a Referral Too

The better people know and trust you, the more likely they are to refer you to others. I always find it amazing that when you really have someone's trust, not only will they refer you, but doing business with them is much easier.

In fundraising, I had so many clients I had built relationships with that when they needed to decide what they were going to sell the next year, they immediately called me and asked for my suggestions. These were people I had gone to dinner with, took in a ballgame with, or played a round of golf with. Sometimes they were people I had simply sat with and listened to.

When spending time with Scott Robbins of Cyberhome I saw him close a $500,000 tack-on sale in just a couple of minutes because of the strong relationship he had with his buyer. He's proof that if you service your clients well, fix their problems, and address any concern they may have, in addition to building that special relationship, you have a customer for life who will gladly refer others to you.

Conclusion

Congratulations! I certainly admire your ability to complete the reading of this book. Now it's time for you to get out there and enjoy your new role as a top-notch sales professional—a professional who can move in the direction of doubling your income in the next two years. It will be challenging, but if you really aim to better yourself in each of the areas we covered in this book, you will come out the other side wiser and richer than ever before.

In my seminars, I often talk about the power of MO (momentum). Momentum is so big in life. Consider this: a large speeding train that has momentum can break through a ten-foot thick brick wall, yet that same train with no momentum would not be able to move a one-inch square piece of wood lying on the track. I promise you, if you read and re-read the chapters in this book, and if you take notes the way I described in chapter one, you will gain momentum and improve. But reading is only half of the equation. The daily discipline to review your notes and practice what you've read is the other half that will make your transformation complete. Additionally, your implementation of the strategies we discussed will be the difference between this book becoming just another one that you put on the bookshelf versus a book that truly changes your life.

Please remember that today your life is the result of your attitude, your actions, and the choices you have made in the past. Your life of tomorrow will be the result of your attitude, your actions, and the choices you make today. If you really want to become a top producing sales professional who can get in every prospect's door and get out with a sale, then choose to keep this book easily accessible and refer to it often.

For more information on sales, sales training, sales consulting, and keynote speeches for your company or organization, you can reach me at **Success Starts Now**, 1-877-589-0606 extension 704, or visit our website at **www.ssnseminars.com**.

I wish you the best of luck in all your future endeavors.

Notes

Recommended Reading

Advanced Sales Strategies by Brian Tracy

Bag the Elephant: How to Win and Keep Big Customers by Steve Kaplan

Creating Sales Velocity by Matthew Ferry

Fish Tales by Stephen Lundin, John Christensen, and Harry Paul

How to Master the Art of Selling by Tom Hopkins

If Success is a Game These are the Rules by Cherie Carter Scott

One Minute for Myself by Spencer Johnson

See You at the Top by Zig Ziglar

Success is a Choice by Rick Pitino

Success is an Inside Job by Lee Milteer

The Question Behind the Question by John Miller

Think and Grow Rich by Napoleon Hill

Walk Like a Giant Sell Like a Madman by Ralph R Roberts

What's Your Excuse by John Foppe

Winning Every Day by Lou Holtz

Index

197

About The Author

Gary has been selling successfully for over twenty-two years. As a college student he worked with the Southwestern Company out of Nashville TN for three summers selling reference books door-to-door, putting in over eighty hours each week. It was here that Gary learned the sales principles and techniques that he now credits for his tremendous sales success over the years. During his tenure with Southwestern he earned over $100,000 in three summers and finished in the top ten out of over three thousand college students worldwide.

Gary recently finished a nineteen year career with Great American Opportunities Inc., a school fundraising company. While there, Gary continued his sales dominance by leading the company in sales for seven of the last ten years out of over two hundred fifty sales reps nationwide. During this time Gary also practiced and perfected his motivational speaking skills, teaching and motivating almost 700,000 students and adults alike.

Over the years, Gary has also sold security systems, excelled in the network marketing arena, and has practiced and studied the real estate profession.

In addition to his own experiences in selling, Gary recently spent a month going out into the field and watching and interviewing several different sales professionals in industries such as financial services, advertising, technology, electronics, pharmaceutical, and many others. From this experience he learned valuable sales lessons that have helped him in creating the material he shares with his audiences. Gary is also an active member in the National Speakers

Association and is always honing his skills by associating and networking with some of the best speakers in the world.

Gary's most recent endeavor is leading a high powered group of individuals in starting a new motivational speaking and training division of the Southwestern Company called Success Starts Now! With the new company, Gary conducts public seminars and sales conferences across the country, as well as offers individual sales training, sales coaching, and sales consulting. For more details, visit *www.ssnseminars.com*.